NO EXCUSES!
WHEN FAILURE IS NO LONGER AN OPTION

WRITTEN BY
EDWARD L. MOORE

www.selfpublishn30days.com

Published by Self Publish -N- 30 Days

Copyright 2017 NO EXCUSES!

All rights reserved worldwide. No part of this book may be reproduced or transmitted in any form or by any means electronic or mechanical, including photocopying, recording or by any information storage and retrieval system without written permission from Edward L. Moore and TNE Training & Consulting.

Printed in the United States of America
ISBN: 978-1981651719

1. Self Help 2. Success-Psychological Aspects
TNE Training & Consulting: NO EXCUSES!

Disclaimer/Warning: This book is intended for lecture and entertainment purposes only. The author or publisher does not guarantee that anyone following these steps will be successful. The author and publisher shall have neither liability responsibility to anyone with respect to any loss or damage cause, or alleged to be caused, directly or indirectly by the information contained in this book.

This book is dedicated to the loving memory of my 2 angels. Velma Rean Williams and Cynthia Marie Jackson. I don't know what I would have done without you two, I love you both and miss you dearly. All I ever wanted to do was make you proud of me. Hopefully when you look down on me you are able to smile knowing that, that which was invested in me is now being manifested. Although I miss you being down here with me, I know that where you are is much better. I can't wait until the day that we are all reunited (which will hopefully be in many years) because your baby boy has work to do. LOL! I will always do my best to represent you both accordingly and I will always carry you with me wherever I go. I love you both.

Until We Meet Again,

Eddie

CONTENTS

INTRODUCTION 1

ACCEPTANCE 5
   1. No Excuses 7
   2. Woe Is Me 17
   3. Self Imposed Limitations 33
   4. Your Feelings Don't Matter 55

ACCOUNTABILITY 63
   5. Time Is Running Out 65
   6. Dream Killers 75

ACTION 97
   7. It All Starts In The Mind 99
   8. Sacrifice For Success 115
   9. Your Biggest Investment 127
   10. Finding Your Niche 137

ADAPTABILITY 147
   11. The Art Of Bouncing Back 149
   12. Progress Is A Process 159

INTRODUCTION

Are you tired of living a mediocre life? Are you tired of living below your standards wishing that your conditions would lead to you being able to achieve everything that you desire? Have you become unsatisfied with your current situation, and feel like there is more for you? Well, if you answered yes to any of these questions, you are just like millions of other people in the same condition around the world. The barrier standing in between most people meeting their goals are the excuses and rationalizations that they make of why they can't get there.

Think about it, how many people have missed opportunities and let their dreams die by the wayside because they saw their obstacles as being more significant than the ability they possessed to conquer them? The truth is, there are times in all of our lives that we have made excuses for why we didn't accomplish the goals that we aspired to accomplish. Some of us have made more excuses than others; however, if you have made a lifestyle of making excuses or made them at different points in your life, the excuses that you made have cost you a lot whether you know it or not. When you don't take ownership and accountability for where you are in your life, you will never become anything more than what your circumstances allow. The power to change your life will always be outside of you, and what will happen is you will end up with unfulfilled dreams, a life that's less than you desired and the pain of living with would've, could've, and should've's.

Most people that give excuses use them as a scapegoat. They use them to evade taking responsibility, and as a result, they end up willfully giving their power over to their circumstances and situations. They feel as if their fate is somehow out of their control which removes them from the responsibility of having to account for the quality of their lives. The truth of the matter is that people often have more power than they realize, but they either doubt the power that they have or are not ready to do the work to operate in it.

In this book, I am going to show you how to take your power back! I am going to show you four principles that will enable you to eliminate excuses from your personal and professional life FOREVER!

As an inspirational speaker and life coach, I have coached countless clients on how to identify and eliminate excuses from their lives. I have made it my life's work to help people overcome self-imposed limitations as I too have had to overcome my internal struggles with complacency and excuse making to get where I am today. That's why I'm so passionate about helping others do the same thing. Through first-hand experience, I know what it's like to be stuck in a place of mediocrity, feeling like there has to be more that life has to offer than what I was experiencing. I also know what it's like to feel as if I'm stuck in the rat race of life while questioning if I will ever make it to the next level. Knowing how hard it was to struggle with living in mediocrity, I felt that it was important for me to share the principles that I have learned with others that have allowed me to overcome complacency.

In this book, I will begin to answer some of the questions that you have about where to start to take control over your life. Hidden within these pages, you will find practical solutions that will empower you to overcome the excuses that have been holding you back.

The content of this book was created to empower you to face life challenges head-on and overcome any obstacle that stands in your way. When you accept the No Excuses philosophy, it will improve the overall quality of your life as you begin to remove barriers that prevent success. In doing so, you will become more self-assured and confident as you realize that you possess the power to create the life that you want. When you shift from the mindset of excuse making to one of accountability, it will allow you to become more productive and efficient which will position you for not only personal but professional advancement.

When you become someone new, everyone connected to you will benefit from the person that you become. You will become better both personally and professionally as a result of taking accountability for the various areas of your life.

I can't begin to tell you how valuable adopting this philosophy has been in my life. I went from a formerly incarcerated high school dropout with a limited skill set to become a highly sought out motivational speaker, author, and life coach. My evolution wasn't an easy one, but one that was achievable once I started to take accountability for my life. After seeing the results of what applying this philosophy did to my own life, I decided to create a platform to share the principles that I had learned with others in hopes that it would help them break out of complacency and take accountability for their own lives. Initially, I started to share this information at trainings with at-risk youth, then eventually with students from all backgrounds. After receiving praise for the impact that the trainings were having, I started receiving referrals to nonprofits and faith-based organizations. As the trainings continued to grow, I began sharing this skill set with businesses and corporations that wanted to build a culture of accountability and increase productivity with their organizations. Needless to say, I have had the benefit of seeing many lives changed by incorporating the habit of eliminating excuse making. I have had the pleasure of seeing people from all walks of life begin to excel educationally, in the workplace and their personal lives as they began to adopt the principles taught in this book.

NO EXCUSES!

In this book, I am not holding back anything, every single principle that I have learned I am going to share with you to empower you to take control over the outcome of your life. By the time you complete this book you will:

1. Develop the self-discipline to meet all of your goals and objectives.
2. Learn how to take full accountability for the outcome of your life.
3. Learn strategies on how to identify your niche, develop it, and create a plan to monetize it.

So, what are you waiting for?

You don't have any more time to wait. You have wasted enough time! There is a saying that says that success is not having all the money in the world but seizing an opportunity when it presents itself. Here is an opportunity right now to break free of the very limitations that have been holding you back and do something about it. Who is counting on you to make this change? Who has been affected by you not being your best self? How could your life be different if you adapted the strategy of accountability in your life? You don't have any more time to waste. The time is NOW! Change is upon you; it's better you seize it and take hold of it!

The information shared in this book is guaranteed to be life changing! The nuggets of wisdom in this book are sure to bless you. You will learn some straightforward yet profound concepts that will prepare you for the next leg of your life. Don't believe me? Open this book up and see for yourself. You will find useful tools that you can apply to every area of your life. It's time to tap into the greatness within you; you deserve it. You deserve to see what your life would look like if you operated in your highest and most authentic self. Join me on this journey of self-discovery and self-mastery on the path to a better you. Your best life is waiting for you! Let's go!!!

PART ONE
ACCEPTANCE

CHAPTER 1
NO EXCUSES

"Excuses are all the reasons that we use to justify why it's ok to fail"

—Edward L. Moore

If I were to ask you, what do you think is the biggest barrier standing between people becoming successful or not becoming successful is, what would you say? You may say a host of things from self-doubt, to lack of determination, to a lack of focus. And while all of these have some element of truth in them, I would argue that the biggest barrier standing between people becoming successful is the excuses that they make for why they can't be.

When you make excuses for your inability to be successful in any area of your life, you have accepted the lie that the power to change your situation or circumstances is outside of you. And as long as you see yourself as powerless in the situation, you will never take the action required to change it.

Everybody says they want to be successful, and I believe that everybody truly wants to be in their heart, but not everyone is ready to do the work that is required to get there, and that's the difference. The work of becoming your best self is hard work, and it takes sacrifices that not everybody is willing to make. Which is why there will always be successful people and those that are not. It's not that the successful people are any more special or even know more than other people. They are simply willing to do the things that others are not willing to do to have the things that others won't have. It's no magic formula; it is really very simple. However, what is not as simple is developing the discipline needed to fulfill your life's dreams.

Usually, those that struggle to develop the self-discipline required to be successful have a whole list of excuses for why they can't do so. You usually hear things like, "I don't have the time," or "I don't have the education," or my favorite, "I don't have the money." In each of these instances, it is not so much what they are up against that prohibits them from being successful as it is a lack of perspective on the situation. What they perceive as a lack of time is really a lack of focus, discipline, and management of their priorities. What they may consider a lack of money may be a lack of creativity, persistence, and determination. Your perspective on things is important, the way you see things is everything. That's why it's of the utmost importance to be truthful with yourself about the excuses that you have allowed yourself to believe. Because once you realize that an excuse is just that, you begin to understand that you hold the power to make a change that can transform your circumstances.

WHAT ARE EXCUSES?

Excuses are mind viruses that we allow to live in our minds rent free that choke the life out of our dreams and make us feel at ease about having a valid reason to fail. For many people, the excuses that they make don't feel like excuses. At least they don't see it that way. In their mind, the barrier standing between them doing what they want to do is a real thing. And let's keep it all the way real; there are times where there are some really valid excuses for why we can't do certain things such as, "I couldn't make it to the gym because there was a snowstorm and the weather advisory suggests that everyone stays in." This is a pretty valid reason for why one might not be able to do what they aspired to do. I'm not here to judge whether your excuses are valid or not. That's not what this is about. I'm simply here to get you to think about, although those barriers are there, what are you going to do about them? Is there any other way to get done what you need to get done? Have you explored all the options? Is there anything else possible that you can do? If you haven't explored every possible option, there may still be a way to get done what you want to get done. When you are chasing a goal, you have to be relentless; you have to stop at nothing until you get what you want. Man listen, where there is a will, there is always a way. If you can't go over it, then go under it, if you can't go under it, go around it, if you can't go around it, bust through it, but no matter what you do, get it done!

Right now, as I write these words, my schedule is so tight that I don't have time for much of anything. But guess what? I'm using my lunch break from coaching to write this content. I don't have a laptop available, so I'm writing on my phone. Over 30% if not more of the content that has been created in this book has been written on my phone because if there is a way to get something done, I'm going to get it done. No excuses! It may not be the most conventional way. Nonetheless, it gets done. If I can sit on social media all day responding to comments and liking post, why can't I use my phone for something more productive like writing a book? Listen, if you want to do something bad enough, you can find a way to do it; you just have to be persistent. Being persistent requires being inconvenienced, it requires getting out of your comfort zone as well as committing to doing what you say you are going to do no matter what opposition comes against you or what is going on.

That's how life is. Life is no cakewalk. Life does not take pity on you or care about all the challenges that you face. Every human faces challenges, but the ones that succeed are the ones that meet the challenges and still find a way to persevere through them. As long as you sit up feeling sorry for yourself, whining about why your life is not what you want it to be, it will continue to be less than you want it to be. You have to take life by the horns and impose your will on life. Life is neutral and is subject to whatever we impose on it. If you take total accountability for your life and do the things that are necessary to succeed, life will submit to you. But if you continue to complain, cry, and make excuses, life will continue to resist you.

When we make excuses, in essence, what we do is place the blame of internal problems on external conditions. Let me elaborate a little further to explain what I mean. When we make excuses, we think that the real barrier is the obstacle that stands in front of us, when in reality it is how we think or see the situation that hinders us. Most obstacles are created in our mind and are only barriers as long as we believe they are. When we begin to see things for what they really are and start doing the hard work of dealing with the self-imposed barriers, we realize that there are far more options available to us than we initially thought. That's why it's so important to continually work on developing your mind because, without a changed mind, you will resort back to the same old behaviors which will make it next to impossible to change.

Change is one of the hardest things to do in the world and requires being pulled and stretched in ways that really challenge you and make you uncomfortable. You can always tell when a person is resistant to change because they will always try to defend their behavior for staying the same.

WHY DO PEOPLE MAKE EXCUSES?

So, why do people make excuses? That's the million-dollar question. People make excuses for a whole host of reasons. I've found that the underlying reason that people make excuses is to attempt to protect themselves from the shame and embarrassment of admitting to failure. Let's be real, who wants to admit that he or she failed at something? When we make excuses, it is how we protect ourselves from feeling the pain and impact of our failed accomplishments. Think about when you question somebody or hold them accountable for what they said they were going to do and they didn't do it, what is the first thing that they do? They try to defend or come up with an excuse for why they didn't do it. It's much easier to deflect the responsibility to something else than it is to accept responsibility when that is not what you are used to doing. In essence, what happens when people make excuses are, they are trying to keep their self-image intact, so they deflect with an excuse to avoid looking bad. But what they don't realize is that when you take accountability for your actions, it empowers you, builds you up, and strengthens your character. There is something to be said about a person that can make a mistake, account for it, and go about the task of fixing it. When people make a habit out of making excuses, they are running from the accountability that is required to change their lives. They are shifting the focus off them and onto other things in order not to accept responsibility for their failures. When you use excuses, that's the easiest way of letting yourself off the hook. Whether you made an excuse because you were doubtful of yourself, you were fearful of the outcome, you were not ready, or you were not motivated, it all boils down to you evading taking action.

CONSEQUENCES OF EXCUSE-MAKING

The implications of making excuses are HEAVY! When I say heavy, I mean heavy. I spent so many years of my life frustrated and mad at the world because my life didn't mirror what I felt that it should be. I was somewhere stuck in between being mad at the world and mad at myself because I couldn't figure this thing called life out. I always had an excuse for why my life wasn't what it should've been. Looking back in hindsight, I now realize that I subconsciously felt as if things should just be handed to me. I was just like so many people that I see trying to take a shortcut in life, thinking that I could put in minimal effort and receive maximum results. Boy, was I in for a rude awakening. It's no wonder I used to walk around with so much frustration and anger; I was angry at myself for not doing what was necessary to be successful and mad at life that it wouldn't just give me what I wanted. As crazy as that sounds, it's people out there right now that just feel like life is supposed to cater to them and give them what they want without putting in the work. They see other people being successful and figure; it looks easy for them, it should be like that for me. That's not how life works. We don't see what the successful people do behind the scenes that contribute to their success. We just see their highlight reel and don't see all the hard work that went into them getting where they are.

The most difficult thing about not taking accountability for where I was at that time in my life, was all the time that I wasted not living up to who I had the potential to be. That's what happens when you avoid taking responsibility, you will never live up to the potential of what you could've been, and that's a scary thing to imagine! People begin to look at you with the side eye and not take you seriously. You start to become the person that's always getting ready to do something, but it never happens. Your integrity becomes in question, and people get to a point where they don't even want to hear what you have to say because every time you open your mouth an excuse is coming out. You begin to lose credibility and before long people start to view you as someone that mouths what they want but never takes action. People love to be around winners, not people that talk the talk but don't walk the walk. There are so many things that we lose when we make excuses that to create a list would take up this whole chapter. That's where your work has to come in. As I will mention later in this chapter, acceptance is the first step in breaking out of the destructive pattern of excuse making. So with that being said, I want you to take an honest assessment of your life and answer the following questions.

What are the excuses that you have made over the course of your life that has cost you? Think about it and be honest with yourself, your future depends on it. Secondly, are you living up to your potential or are you just a shadow of what you could be if you stopped making excuses for what you're not and tapped into what you are? Lastly, how much time have you wasted not living the life that you are capable of? Time is running out, and the graveyard is filled with plenty of excuse makers that never realized their potential. Will you be one of them? Or will you take the rest of your life that you have left and make the most of it? Let's take you out of the equation for a minute and let's think about the people that you are responsible for and those that are connected to you. Should they have to suffer because you couldn't dig deep enough to keep it real to yourself and admit that you have been making excuses? And that you have not been operating in your best self and as a result, your life is not what it could be?

When people ask me why I go so hard, it's because I know what it's like to feel like a complete failure, to have my children have a need and not be able to fulfill it because my finances won't allow it. I know what it's like to see my sister go through a horrific health situation and be threatened to not get adequate care because of finances and her life being dependent on the treatment. I know what it's like to go in my own personal space and cry like a baby because I'm not able to provide my grandmother with all the resources that she needed to be comfortable as she started aging after she took care of us our entire life. The excuses you make are bigger than you. You have a responsibility to be your best self. First of all, you owe it to you. Secondly you owe it to your family, and lastly, you owe it to anybody that God had called you to be a blessing to.

You will never become who you want to be while you're making excuses, you will never grow as a person when making excuses, and ultimately you will never know what your life could have been. Are you ok with that? Will you just try to sweep it under the rug and try to get lost in distractions to not think about it? Are you hoping that it goes away? Well, I'm here to tell you, my friend, it's not going away until you begin to address the issues that are holding you back; they will continue to haunt you like a scary movie before bed.

THE SOLUTION (THE 4 A'S)

Don't be alarmed; there is hope. As I have gone through the journey of transforming my life, I have learned some very valuable strategies and principles that have allowed me to overcome the habit of excuse making and achieve goals that I had only dreamed about before. The principles that I will share with you are ones I didn't find in a book or learn in a classroom. I discovered them through first-hand experience, so I know that they work. I have seen what they have done in my life, and I'm confident that they can do the same thing for you if applied. The philosophy that I'm referring to is TNE's philosophy to eliminate excuses. It's called the 4 A's. The 4 A's are some very simple principles that you can apply to any area of your life where you need to remove excuses.

STRATEGIES TO ELIMINATE EXCUSES 4A'S

1. ACCEPTANCE - (Acknowledgment of my participation in failure) - To address any problem in your life, the first thing that you have to do is admit that you have a problem. The first thing that they ask you to do when you go to most recovery programs is admitting that you have a problem. Why? Because if you don't acknowledge that you have a problem, then you don't have anything to work on. In this case, the problems that we are referring to are excuses. If you don't keep it real with yourself about the areas that you have been making excuses, then you will never overcome them. The first stop on the journey to eliminate excuses from your life is being honest with yourself that you make them. We are taking the focus off everybody else and focusing it solely on you! This is about you. This is the moment of truth. This is the moment where you accept the parts of yourself that are hard to face so that you can begin doing the work to become a better you. Acceptance is the first step to change and your starting point.

2. ACCOUNTABILITY - (Taking ownership over the outcome of your life) - Now that you have accepted the fact that you have been making excuses, you have to be accountable for them. Accountability is not only owning up to what you have done but also accepting responsibility to change it. Accountability is preparing yourself to do whatever it is that you need to do to correct the problems that you have identified in your life. That's some hard work because you may have to face some things that are not so pleasant about yourself like I mentioned earlier, but it's so worth it. When you become accountable, you don't allow yourself to evade responsibility for your role in any situation, but you take full ownership over what happened as well as what needs to change. Accountability is the last step of preparation before you take action to change.

3. **ACTION - (Paying the price for the life that you want daily)** – Ok, so you have accepted that excuses are a problem, you have committed in your heart to do something about them. What's left? Now it's time to take some action. It's time to do something about them. It's time to make some changes and account for every area of your life. It's time to operate in the reality that if your life is going to be anything, it is up to you to make it be. This is where the rubber meets the road and where most people never follow through on their commitment or don't develop the discipline to act consistently on what they know that they should be doing. This is not for the faint of heart. This is the place where the grinders grind, and the overcomers overcome. This is where the victory is won, and lives are changed. Action is doing whatever it is that you need to do regardless of being scared, not feeling motivated, or not having the support that you need. It is a self-commitment, and you have to follow through with your commitment long after the feeling that you said it in is gone. It's time to act!

4. **ADAPTABILITY - (Finding the flexibility to survive life's storms)** - And last but definitely not the least the last A is adaptability. Adaptability or resilience is the understanding that everything is not going to go as planned always. It's the understanding that you have to be flexible and adjust as you learn along the journey. My personal experience when I start working on anything is that I experience things both good and bad that I didn't anticipate. Let me correct myself, nothing is really bad; it's all about learning lessons of what went well and what didn't. One of the most beautiful parts of the process of dream chasing is learning from all of the different experiences. It is an unpredictable journey and life will throw you some curve balls, but as long as you are flexible, you can bounce back from anything and apply what you learned to readjust and keep moving towards your goals. Always remember, there are no good or bad experiences, just lessons on what to do and what not to do on your journey to success.

HOW THE BOOK IS WRITTEN

This book contains 12 chapters full of life-changing content that will empower you to live an excuse-free life. The book is broken down into four sections to thoroughly examine each of the 4A's in greater detail. Section one is entitled **ACCEPTANCE (Acknowledgment of my role in failure)** - This section contains four chapters that teach practical strategies on how to identify and accept the areas of your life that you have been making excuses. In this section, we look at the role we play in our own failure when we refuse to take accountability for the outcome of our lives.

In the next two chapters of section 2 entitled **ACCOUNTABILITY (Taking ownership over the outcome of your life)** - We discuss the importance of taking complete ownership of your personal and professional goals. In these two chapters, you will learn simple strategies on how to take accountability for the outcome of your life.

In section 3 which is entitled **ACTION (Paying the price for the life that you want daily)** - It contains four chapters where we will share with you some strategies that are essential to taking action steps to create the life that you want. There are tips on how to prepare yourself mentally for the challenges ahead as well as a section dedicated to teaching you how to identify your gift, develop it, and how to create a plan to monetize it.

Lastly, in section 4 which is **ADAPTABILITY (Finding the flexibility to survive life's storms)** - We will discuss the importance of having patience along the journey of dream chasing as well as remaining flexible and learning from each experience to make the necessary adjustments needed to reach your life's goals.

CHAPTER 2
WOE IS ME

"You're only a victim to the degree of what your perception allows."

—Shannon L. Elder

Life is full of some interesting turns, sometimes in life things will feel like they are going very well for you and other times it will feel like everything's falling apart. Nobody, I repeat nobody is immune to the trials and tribulations of life. Living a life free of problems and challenges is impossible. That is simply not the way life is set up. Traveling along this journey that we call life, we will all experience some things that test our resolve. As unfair as this seems, there is simply no way around it. Although we will all experience challenges, they don't have to defeat us. What's important, is how we choose to respond to the challenges that we all will inevitably face. Everybody deals with problems; some just choose to deal with them differently from others. Some people face challenges going in with the mindset that they will find a way to overcome this while others face their challenges with a defeated mindset. How you view what you go through can determine whether you will overcome it, or if it will overcome you. I want to take a few seconds to explore a particular aspect of a defeated mindset that is very detrimental to your success. It is what I like to refer to as the "Woe Is Me" or victim mentality. The victim mentality is when you develop a mindset that makes you feel that you have little to no control over your life. It's the belief that the challenges that you face in life are due to the actions of something or someone else, and that you are powerless to change them. When you look at life through the lens of a victim, life seems unfair, and you believe that you are prone to bad things always happening to you. It's a mindset that says life is negative, change is beyond my control, and that I should be given sympathy for all the bad things that are happening in my life. At its core, the victim mentality is a mindset that says so many bad things have happened and will continue to happen to me in my life, why should I even try to fight it? The victim mindset is the ultimate acceptance of failure! Let's take a look at how the victim mindset plays out in the lives of its victims.

THE MINDSET OF THE VICTIM

HELPLESSNESS

Have you ever felt like just giving up? Like no matter what you did, things would never get better? Feeling like, why should I even continue to try to fight? If you have ever felt like that, you are not alone. I can recall the feeling all too well of feeling like I was powerless to create change in my life. Feeling like control of my life was outside of myself and in the hands of some other external force. In my own mind, I was a prisoner of my circumstance, one with very few options. But the truth of the matter is that I always had control of my life. It may not have felt like it, but the power was always inside of my hands. You see, when we feel powerless, we can begin to accept those feelings of helplessness as absolute truth. And the reality is that just because you feel helpless doesn't mean that those feelings are rooted in truth. As a matter of fact, it's the exact opposite of the truth; it's a lie. It is just a feeling. Many people let how they feel dictate their entire life and make permanent decisions based on a feeling that may change in the future. They perceive their feelings to be the truth, so in essence, they become truth because as a man thinks so is he. And their lives become what they perceive them to be. It becomes a self-fulfilling prophecy. When you begin to believe you are powerless, you will never make any attempts to get out of your defeated state because you believe there are no options. People give up in the face of adversity when they feel like there is nothing they can do to change their lives. They passively surrender and allow themselves to be subjected to whatever fate life throws at them. They give up on hope and yield their power to change to the feelings of powerlessness that are not even true. It's disheartening to think about all the people that gave up on life and stopped fighting when they really had enough in them to overcome whatever they were going through. There is nothing that you can't overcome! There is nothing that you can't make it through! You just have to stay in the fight long enough to weather the storm and make it through.

THE PITY PARTY

People that see themselves as victims often feel sorry for themselves. Not only do they feel sorry for themselves, but they also want others to feel sorry for them too. You see, them receiving pity validates that the responsibility of their current state is not their fault. And while there may be some things that have happened to us that are outside of our control, the responsibility of the quality of our life lies with us. Seeking validation from others to justify why we are not able to get where we want to go in life is a very dangerous place to be in. When you look for others to empathize with your failure, you are in essence asking people to ally with you against your own success because to pat you on the back and tell you it's ok you are not where you want to be is to support your demise. And while having somebody to validate your struggle or hardship may feel good in the immediate, it does nothing to push you towards your ultimate goal in the long run. All it simply does is make you feel good about not achieving your goal, and that's not to anybody's benefit. Rather than having someone validate why you couldn't do something, it's important to have someone to hold you accountable for what you could do.

THE EVERYBODY'S OUT TO GET ME MENTALITY

As crazy as it sounds, most people that subscribe to the victim mentality feel as if everything and everyone is conspiring against their failure. They feel that people have negative intentions towards them and actually don't want to see them get ahead. Most of the time the things that they perceive are against them are not even true. It's simply how they perceive things to be. With all the people in the world, how did the world come to conspire about sabotaging your life? But as irrational as it seems, these feelings seem very real when you are overwhelmed by conditions that are less than you would want them to be. As I work with some of my clients in the capacity of a Life Coach, I'm all too familiar with this mindset. Many of them feel that not only people but systems are also conspiring against them to see them fail. I have heard everything from "nobody wants to give me a job" to "good things never happen to people like me," and the saddest thing about this mindset is that they actually believe it's true. There is so much focus on the conspiracy going on against them that they never grasp the concept of how much power is actually in their hands to transform their situation. While there may be some truth to systems being in place that were created to marginalize certain groups of people, I'm big on personal accountability and responsibility. Because the truth of the matter is, some things are out of our control to change. They must be fought on a bigger level, but many things are within our control like what we do with our personal lives despite the systems that were put in place for our failure. Even if everybody in the world was conspiring against your failure, the only way that could happen is if you waved the white flag and surrendered to their plan for your life. In life, there will always be opposition. There will always be people that don't want to see you get ahead, there will still be haters, but the only thing that matters is what you do with your God-given abilities. Your will to win has to be bigger than any opposition that is coming against you.

GOING FROM VICTIM TO VICTOR

TAKE ACCOUNTABILITY (ACKNOWLEDGMENT)

The very first step to overcoming the victim mentality is taking responsibility for wherever you may find yourself in life. Nothing and nobody has more control over your life than you do. No matter what situation that you may find yourself in, you can influence the direction of your life. The problem is that people like to scapegoat and play the blame game and absolve themselves from all responsibility for areas they need to change or address. Changing can be hard especially when you are used to doing things a certain way for a long time. You guys know I'm telling the truth. Have you ever had something that you had to be accountable for changing, that you weren't quite ready to change? That is one of the hardest things to do ever! The things that we need to change most in our lives are often holding us back from the quality of life that we really desire. Wheeeewwwww! That was a good one! That blessed me even writing it. But that's what the truth does for you. It sets you free when you accept it. You see, the first step to change is to first admit that you have a problem. To overcome the victim mentality, you have to be honest with yourself and take ownership of the fact that you have been operating from that place. The reason that it is so important to take ownership of the problem that you have is this; if you don't own the fact that you need to make some changes, then you rob yourself of the opportunity to do so because the power to do so is not in your hands. Did you get that? For you to change, there has to first be an acknowledgment of a need to change followed by a desire and then action. The longer that you evade responsibility, the longer it will take for your life to become what you want it to be. And if you never take accountability for where you want to be your life will never change. You see this is one of those things in life where it is you against you; nobody else can do this for you! So, you have to take responsibility because nobody else is going to change your life but you. Nobody has a vested interest in the outcome of your life the way you do. There may be people that love you and want to see you do well, but at the end of the day, you have to live out the consequences or rewards of the decisions that you make. So, what are you gonna do? Are you going to take full responsibility for where your life is? Or, are you going to allow everything that you have been through to serve as your reason for why you can't be what you want to be and have what you want to have? The choice is yours. Choose wisely; your future depends on it.

WHAT ARE YOU WAITING FOR? (DESIRE)

In order for you to start to desire change in your life, you have to first see a reason compelling enough for you to want to change. Part of acknowledgment is to accept that some of the ways that we have been doing things have not been working. There are two ways that people begin to desire change. It is either they get to a point where they are sick and tired of being sick and decide to change or either some unforeseen life event, or circumstance forces them to change. Either way, change is inevitable, so if you know that at some point in your life that you will face a season when you know that you will need to change, wouldn't you want to be in control of the decision to change? I mean, think about it, does it make more sense to sit back and wait for something to happen to say hey I guess I better get myself together? Or does it make more sense to accept the fact that there are some things in your life that you could be doing better and then decide to act on them make more sense? The former is reactive while the latter is proactive, which is what we want to strive to be. We want to be proactive about all of the areas of our lives that require change. Who wants to sit around waiting for something to force you out of your comfort zone to create change? I know I don't, but I have been there before, even as it relates to my own health. About 5-6 years ago, I began to pick up a little weight. I didn't think anything of it, I just attributed it to my bad eating habits. One day, I went in for a routine checkup, and the doctor ordered me to do some blood work which is standard for a checkup. I did the labs, and my sugar levels came back elevated, and they told me that I was pre-diabetic. So, a short time later I went on an all-out health kick where I lost about 40 lbs. So, as you can imagine after losing 40lbs, I was very proud of my results. I was looking good and feeling good, and then I started to lose focus. Over the course of time, I began to get comfortable and began to take my foot off the pedal and slowly but surely, I gained back every pound that I had lost. Sometime later, I went back to the doctor to get a random checkup. The doctor ordered me to take some more labs and guess what? I ended up getting diagnosed with type 2 diabetes. Unlike before where I had the option to take better care of myself, I was now forced to. I have since gone on to lose weight and get my diabetes totally controlled with diet and exercise, but this is a situation that could have been totally prevented. This situation taught me a very valuable lesson, one that I will have to live with for the rest of my life. As a result of not acting upon what I knew I should have acted upon at the time in which I should have, I am now forced to take better care of my health, but that is something I could have decided to do on my own initially and avoid becoming a diabetic. You see, that is what many of us do, we wait until we get the diagnosis or wait until things are at a point where you have no choice but to change before taking some action. At some point in life, we have to develop the self-determination and motivation to do the things that we know that we need to do before being provoked to. In deciding to be proactive, you can determine when change will happen for you, while being reactive, the only option that you have is how you will respond to the change that is being forced on you. For a second, I would like you to consider a couple of questions. In what areas of your life could you be more proactive with the things that you need to change? What things have you been allowing to linger that are standing between you and where you want to be? I strongly encourage you to, to acknowledge the areas of your life that require change while you have an opportunity, make a commitment and decide to change and then follow through with some action before you are forced to like I was.

DESTROYING THE VICTIM MENTALITY (ACTION)

Overcoming the victim mentality can be challenging but not as hard as you may think. It will require you keeping it real with yourself about some things that may be hard for you to accept, but it will make you better in the long run. Acceptance of the fact that you have been operating as a victim is the starting point of your work, but that's not where it ends. To overcome this mentality, it will require changing your perspective and viewing life through a different lens. In this portion of the chapter, I will share with you five keys that have helped me overcome the victim mentality and take control over my life.

1. **Humble Yourself To Accept The Truth**- One of the hardest things to do in life is receiving critical feedback about yourself or accepting things about yourself that you need to change. It almost feels like an attack on your character or that you are being viewed as less than. But the reality is, a person that can't take feedback or even be honest with themselves about the things that they need to change will never grow. So many people get caught up trying to defend their image that they don't see the blessing in being made aware of areas that they need to change that would make their life better. They miss out on an opportunity to improve themselves because their pride has them more focused on defending their flaws than accepting the need to change. That's why it's important to humble yourself. When you humble yourself, you realize that you don't know everything and that maybe some areas of your life could use some improvement. You also realize that you don't have to defend yourself against everything. Humbling yourself is the first step because in order to receive the truth, you must be in a place to accept it. I remember when my life first started to change for the better. It was changing for the better, and I didn't even recognize it because it didn't feel like it at the time. It was September of 2000, and I had found myself incarcerated for the third time in my life. This time was different though because I

found myself jailed for some things I hadn't done, but I was there. The district attorney fought hard to send me to prison but as an act of divine intervention, I got sentenced to a year in the San Francisco county jail under the stipulation that I had to attend and complete a program called Resolve To Stop The Violence Project or have all of my back time taken back and do three years in prison. The program was for violent offenders that is designed to hold clients accountable for the violence that they have inflicted on themselves and others. The program was very strenuous and many of the participants didn't complete it because they just couldn't handle the rigors of the program. You have to attend classes daily from 7:00 in the morning to 8:00 at night. As you can imagine, when I came to the program, I wasn't feeling it. I walked into the program that first day disgusted that I would have to be subjected to this type of structure for the next year of my life. Everybody was sitting around kumbaya style talking about their problems and giving each other feedback. I was resistant to the whole idea especially given the fact that I was there for a crime that I didn't commit. I had a very hard exterior, and I didn't want to hear anything that they were talking about. I planned to go into the program and fake it just enough to get past the program. But an interesting thing happened to me. As I was sitting in class observing the information presented, I started to hear some information that resonated with me about the way I did things that had an impact on myself as well as other people. I really started to see myself within the information that I was learning in the group, so at that point I could've continued to reject the information even though it was true, or I could humble myself and accept the truth about the areas of my life that could use some change. So obviously, I chose the latter. And let me tell you that this is the best decision that I ever made in my life. I went on to open myself up to all of the information that was presented in the program and did so well that when I got out, I got offered an internship to the same program that I was a client in. Six months later, I got offered a full-time position to the same program. That was now sixteen years ago. And the first decision to accept the truth has led me to several more professional opportunities over the years including the one that I have now, which is to work as a Life Coach for the City of Oakland where I coach young men that have been perpetrators as well as victims of violence. But even more than the professional opportunities that came from that experience, humbling myself back in 2000 has made me a better human being. I can now easily accept the areas of my life that require change without being in denial, blaming or minimizing. Just the ability to do that has allowed me to overcome many of the obstacles that were holding me back and transform my life into what you see today.

2. **Acknowledge The Need For You To Take Responsibility**- No matter what is going on live life whether good, bad, or indifferent always keep it real with yourself. Always be honest enough with yourself to acknowledge the truth. As painful as it may be allowing the light of truth into your life, it will position you to address the areas of your life that need improvement. Like I mentioned in the story earlier, I could have totally denied the fact that I needed to change like I saw so many of my peers do in the program. Or I could've done what I did which was accepted the truth. I'm so very thankful that I saw the importance of doing so even at that young age of my life because when I look at what became of my life and the lives of those that didn't, the difference is day and night. The first time I really started to become aware of how impactful that decision was when I became staff at the program. I saw some of my peers that I was in the program with cycle in and out of jail regularly ask me for help to get them into the program to aid them with their cases. These were the same guys that teased me for taking the program so

seriously. They said things like, "You wasn't programming on the street," which was their way of saying why are you trying to change? Why are you trying to switch up? To do things differently than how you were conditioned to is frowned upon in many environments, but each individual must make decisions that are best for them and their lives. That's what I chose to do for myself. I was simply tired of living beneath my privilege, I saw an opportunity to change, and I took it. I'm no different from them. The only difference is that I decided to acknowledge the need for me to take responsibility for the areas of my life that needed change. Many of them are now deceased or over the years have continued to cycle in and out of jail and my life has continued to get better and better. This is no knock on them by any stretch of the imagination; I only point this out to say that the decisions that you make can alter the whole course of your life.

3. **Acknowledge Your Own Power**- To move beyond the victim mindset, it's important to shift your thinking from the things that have happened to you to what you have the power to change. You have to train yourself to think differently especially if your mind has been conditioned to see the negative in every situation. You have power within you that you couldn't even imagine. You can solve the problem and overcome almost any situation that you face. However, if you don't see the problem, it will lay dormant within you. Look at it like this; I equate having power within you that is lying dormant to having a backup generator and being in the midst of a power outage and not plugging it in. You can access the power that is available to you, but because you are not plugged into the source, it just goes unused. And instead of the power being used to bless your life, you sit in the dark unnecessarily suffering because you are not using what's available to you. You have to believe that you possess a power within you even if it's not clear what that quite looks like. It's imperative that you believe in you. It's essential that you believe

in your own ability. The key to tapping into that power is first to realize that it is there at your disposal to be used at any time. Once you become aware of it and begin to use it, your life will change dramatically. I have an exercise for you just to test this theory out to see if it works. The next time you face an obstacle that seems like it's doomed to failure, I want you to instead of thinking it's hopeless, take out a pad and a pen and brainstorm every possible option on fixing the situation. After that, I want you to apply what you came up with and see if there is a different result. You might be surprised at the difference.

4. **Accept What Happened And Keep It Moving**- Sometimes in life things happen to us that are outside of our control. You didn't do anything that warranted it, it just happened, and it was unfortunate. I think it's safe to say we all have at least one experience like that in our life. And while it is not your fault what happened to you, it is your responsibility for what happens to the outcome of the rest of your life. Some people are literally stuck in mental prisons that are angry, jaded, and frustrated over what somebody did to them in their past. And while I'm not saying it was ok or dismissing it, I'm saying that you have a responsibility to live your best life despite what happened to you. You could hold on to the poison of anger and resentment and let it affect the quality of your life, or you can let it go. The people that did things to us have gone on to live their lives and probably don't even think about us, but we still carry the baggage of these past hurts. We can't change the past and go back in time, all we can do is deal with the present. All we can do is play our part to ensure that our future is better than our past. It would be in your best interest to let the things that happened to you go. It doesn't mean that you let them off the hook or excuse their behavior. It means that you love you enough to release yourself from the weight of the previous hurt in your life. My life

wasn't a conventional one by any stretch of the imagination; I am a product of the union of a drug-addicted mother and a father that has never claimed me until in recent years. With all of that, I could have had plenty of excuses for why my life is not where it could've been if I had a mother that cared and nurtured me or a father that was in my life. But the truth of the matter is that none of that matters. Yes, people did me wrong, yes, my conditions were challenging to overcome. But I had two choices; either I could let the circumstances that I was born into define my life, or I could say despite all of that I am going to use those experiences to fuel my passion to make my life be everything that it should be. I just refuse to be a victim of my circumstance. No matter what cards you were dealt and no matter how bad the hand is, it's the only hand that you have to play. So, despite your upbringing, despite who wronged you, and despite not having support, you can make your life become everything that you want it to be when you let the pain of the past go; use that focus to move towards your purpose.

5. **Walk In The Truth Of A New Story**- To walk in newness, you have to change the story that you tell yourself. It may be hard initially because you are used to thinking negatively, but over the course of time, it will get easier. For me, I had to literally make myself think what I wanted to think because my natural default was negative stinking thinking. Even now, if I'm not intentional about the things that I allow in my mind as well as what I think, my mind will go to its default. You have to be intentional about what you allow yourself to believe even if you don't feel like it. It is a full-time job to direct your mind in the direction that you want it to go but absolutely necessary to be victorious in life. You have to see yourself in your mind's eye as the person that you want to become because if you don't change how you see yourself, it will be tough to change the narrative in your mind about who you are and what you can do.

Look at my situation for example. If I had continued to look at myself as a formerly incarcerated ex-offender from the streets born to a drug-addicted mother and a father that didn't claim me, I would say that the outlook for a person from those beginnings are very limited. Never in my wildest dreams did I think that I would be a Motivational Speaker, Author, and Life Coach coming from where I come from. I had to begin to change the way that I saw myself before anybody else would see me differently. Not only change the way that I saw myself but start to walk in that confidence. Walk in the confidence that I fully possessed the talent and skill set within me to do everything thing that I wanted. You can do the same thing too. In shifting your thinking about yourself, you would be amazed at the things that you can accomplish. In this year alone, I set out to achieve three primary goals. The first was to complete this book, the second was to become a certified Life Coach, and lastly to create my proprietary "No Excuses" training where I go in and teach businesses and corporations how to eliminate excuses and institute a culture of accountability to increase efficiency and productivity within their organizations. By year's end, I will have completed all three. Not bad for a formerly incarcerated drug dealer, huh? Change the narrative of yourself in your mind, and you will change your life!

If there is anything that I can leave you with, it's always to remember that you are not a victim of any situation or circumstance. Things may have happened to you that you didn't warrant, but you still possess the power to direct your life in the direction that you want it to go. I want to take the time to acknowledge that some of the things that you have been through have left a huge impact on you, but at the end of the day, you are still responsible for the outcome of your life. It is my sincerest desire that you take everything that you have been through and use it as fuel to propel you into your future. Every bad experience doesn't have to result in a bad outcome, just look at what happened to me. I was able to take the experience of getting incarcerated for an offense that I didn't even commit and use it to transform my entire life. I'm not special; I'm no different from you. You can do the same thing. Things that were meant to harm you can be turned around for your good! The difference between being a victim and a victor is how you see the situation. Your days of being a victim are over; it's time to walk in the victory that is before you.

CHAPTER 3
SELF-IMPOSED LIMITATIONS

*"Believe in your infinite potential.
Your only limitations are those you set upon yourself."*

—Roy T. Bennett

Are you living limitless or do you doubt that there are endless possibilities out there for you? Do you believe that you can do all things, or have you put a cap on your abilities? Do you see yourself as being worthy of achieving greatness or do you secretly believe there is a glass ceiling for you? These are some daunting questions that I think we must all ask ourselves at some point if we are not experiencing the level of success that we aspire to achieve in life. If you are not where you want to be in life or feel like there is another level that you would like to reach that you haven't, it may be time to have a real honest conversation with yourself and examine what is holding you back. Nine times out of ten, the answer will in some shape, form or fashion be related to the way you think. There are far too many people that are not where they want to be in life, and the only thing standing between them getting where they want to go is the belief that they can't get there. The sad thing is that a lot of people are capable of more than they realize but no matter how many talents and gifts that they have, it means nothing if they don't believe that they are capable of achieving what they aspire to do. You can encourage them, tell them what you see in them, but until they can see it for themselves, any efforts to move forward will be hindered. You can never operate beyond your vision of yourself. So, where you are today in your life is in direct relation to how you see yourself.

That's why the first step in achieving any goal is conditioning the mind to believe you can do it. Because if you don't, at some point, those debilitating thoughts of fear and doubt will creep up on you and strangle the life out of your dreams. Success has to start internally first before it can manifest itself externally. To put it in layman's terms, you have to become what you desire to be mentally and emotionally long before you become it physically. You have to visualize yourself being what you want to be in your mind's eye to bring it to fruition. This is why you have so many people go after their dreams and desires and end up giving up, they have accepted the lie that they are not good enough, they don't have what it takes, or it's going to be too hard. Whatever the reason is, the belief that they cannot possess what they want out of life permanently disqualifies them.

DON'T BELIEVE THE HYPE
ACCEPTING THE LIES

As somebody that struggled much of my life with believing in myself and my abilities, I know firsthand how hard it can be when your mind has been programmed for failure. Not only did I doubt my abilities, but I also struggled internally with if I was truly worthy. So much so, that there are several things that I just didn't even attempt to go after because of how I really felt about myself. By all appearances, I appeared to be very confident, but deep down on the inside, I had a lot of self-doubt and insecurity. Maybe it was because I never had anybody to build me up with positive affirmations. Or perhaps it was because I grew up in an environment where there were not many successful people outside of illegal activity. Or maybe it was because

I accepted the limitations that were set for me by others. Whether it was because of limitations that I set in my own mind or those set by others, I had accepted the lie. What lie you might ask? I'm talking about the lie that I wasn't good enough, that I didn't have what it took, that somebody else was more deserving of the best life had to offer than me. I believed that others were more intelligent that they were more gifted and more talented. All the while I was overlooking my own gifting and abilities never tapping into the greatness that was inside of me. It has taken many years to get to a place where I was able to overcome the self-imposed limitations that were holding me back. It has taken years of very intentional work and personal self-development. Most people don't even realize that they are being programmed for failure that it happens so subtly. Somewhere along the line, we start to accept the lies that we are not good enough or we don't truly have what it takes to have what we want to have and be what we want to be. Often the messaging is not even in the form of actual words, often our surroundings and the things that we are exposed to on a daily basis speak to us louder than any words can.

BOUNDING OF SURROUNDINGS

Environment is everything; your environment can either position you for success or condition you for failure. There are very few individuals that have more impact on their environment than their environment has over them. I know this to be true in my own life. Back when I was in high school, I was a terrible student not because I was unintelligent, but simply because I was unfocused and didn't have anybody holding me accountable. So, as a result, I never excelled academically. I came home to an environment where there was no significant emphasis on education, and I was allowed to do as I pleased. My environment was full of distractions which at the time I valued more than education. I was caught up in the now more than the later. You know the age-old battle between instant gratification and long-term fulfillment that many of us face. I was influenced by what was immediately around me. In Rome, you do as the Romans do, so a lot of the things that were being done in my environment I began doing. But an amazing thing happened to me in the summer of my freshman year going into my sophomore year in high school. I applied and got accepted into a program called the Upward Bound. The Upward Bound is a college prep program that affords high school kids the opportunity to live on a college campus and take college courses over the summer as they prepare you for college. By all accounts, I shouldn't have even been allowed into the program, but I wrote an essay so compelling of why I should be allowed into the program that they decided to give me an opportunity to attend for the summer. As you may imagine, I came to the program with the intention of doing things the way that I had always done them. It was my goal to do as little as possible to get by to stay in the program. I was more concerned with the young ladies that were in the program than I was the actual academic opportunities that were being offered. Although I had intentions of skating my way through the program, I quickly found out that it wasn't an option. My first day in the program I began to understand very quickly that there were high expectations of us and that we would be held accountable for being our very best. This was different for me. Initially, I was a little bit resistant and tried to find shortcuts to doing things the way that was requested of us, but soon found that to be futile. You see, unlike before where I was able to do as I chose, I now had some structure put in place. We had designated times in which we had to study and do homework. We had staff checking our homework and making sure we completed it daily. Before any recreation was allowed, your primary objective had to be met which was your school work. For the very first time in my life, the kid known for getting F's and D's was now an A and B student. What had changed about me? I was now in an environment where excellence was demanded of me. I was in an environment of structure and accountability which allowed me to tap into the side of myself that was fully capable of excelling academically given the right environment. I'm merely using myself as an example to say that environments can have a significant impact on you. It is imperative to evaluate your environment to determine whether it is conducive to where you are trying to go or not. If the answer is no, you must find a way to surround yourself with people that will not only support and encourage you, but that will hold you accountable as well. I can hear some of you saying now, "But I don't have anybody to support me." Well, my suggestion to you my friend is to seek out what you want and align yourself with people that are going in the same direction as you. Once you begin to operate in the fullness of who you are, you won't have to look hard because greatness attracts greatness.

CAN'T OPERATE BEYOND YOUR VISION OF YOURSELF

The mind is a very powerful thing. The mind can take you to great heights or keep you bound from achieving anything notable. It is amazing how two people can be brought up in the same exact conditions, given the equal opportunities and one will use their mind to transform their lives, and the other forfeit their God-given genius because of unbelief in their abilities. When we see ourselves as being less than we are, it becomes a self-fulfilling prophecy. If you believe that you can only go so far, subconsciously you will shut down once you get to whatever you feel your limit is. Let me give you an example. I will use running as an analogy. My brother who is to remain nameless had long since given up on his ability to run or do anything with his legs. In his mind, he felt that he had bad knees and if he did anything which required running or using his legs, he would re-injure them. So as a result, what he believed about his legs kept him from even trying to run. It was like pulling teeth to try to engage him around running or exercising with his legs. Every time he would decline stating the same thing that his knees had been bad since high school and that it was an area of his life that he had given up on. To my surprise, I invited him to come hiking with me, and he accepted. Within 2 hikes, he was leaving me in the dust. Trust me these hikes are not just a walk in the park. Every hike is a minimum of 6-7 miles and upwards of 10-12 miles. So, the more he began to hike, the more he started to gain confidence. And then something magical happened. A mutual friend of ours and fitness guru invited my brother for a jog around Lake Merritt and wouldn't take no for an answer. To our surprise, my brother accepted with his new-found confidence. What happened next was beyond everybody's expectations. My brother was running and keeping up with those that had been running regularly for years. Even to this day when we run he usually beats me. I have to put this disclaimer out there though, he is tall and has exceptionally long legs. But in all seriousness, the very thing he had told himself that he could no longer do over 2 decades ago, not only was he doing but doing at a high level. I think the day of my brother's first run marked a special day for him. The day was a day of confirmation for him. I believe that day signified that when you expand your boundaries and believe in your abilities, your belief will take you to places that you never imaged. Within a year's time, the same guy that had given up on his legs ended up completing his first marathon. In life, the only limitations that truly exist are the ones that are in your mind.

REMOVING THE BARRIERS
YOU DON'T KNOW UNLESS YOU TRY

I need you to do me a huge favor. When I say I need you to do me a favor, I really need you to do me a favor. Better yet I need you to do YOU a favor. I need you to examine everything that you have somehow believed that you couldn't do. And I need you to ask yourself a very critical question. I need you to ask yourself, how do you know you can't do something if you have never tried it before? Even if you have tried and didn't succeed the first time does that mean you're a failure? Does that mean that you can't learn to do what you aspire to do? No, not at all, it just means that you have tried something and didn't get it right on the first time. It simply means that you have found out a way that doesn't work. The problem is that we get so discouraged by things not happening the way we want them to right away that we let discouragement set in and start to believe the lies that we are not capable of completing our goals. What's even worse is to conclude that you can't do something that you have never tried. Maybe you fear failing, perhaps you have never done it before, or you don't have anybody to show you how to do it. None of these excuses are valid because all they do is serve as crutches to aid you in your decision not to try to do the things that you may find out that you are fully capable of doing. It's just like the analogy of my brother, imagine if he didn't allow himself to be pushed outside of his comfort zone, he would have never experienced what his legs were truly capable of let alone run a marathon. The same rings true for us if you never attempt to go after what it is that you want, you will never know what you are capable of having! Imagine a life wasted playing it safe, staying in our comfort zone, and going to our grave as untapped potential. Being literally at the end of our days with the haunting questions of what if I had only tried? What could I have been? How could my life have turned out? You see, we are all given only one life, and we are all given free will of how we will make use of it. Whether we use the time that we have allotted on this earth to maximize every second to build the lives we want, or we allow doubt and fear to render us incapable of being what we want. The choice is always ours. But the truth of the matter is that we all are without excuse because everything that you need to succeed is already inside of you! So right now, this very moment, I need you to be honest with yourself. I need you to be honest about the things that you have allowed yourself to believe that you can't do and do this very simple exercise, simply try. Just make an honest effort to do the very thing that you have convinced yourself that you couldn't do but secretly desire to do. I need you to go into it with the confidence that you are fully capable of anything that you put your mind to. And what you find out may blow your mind.

HOPE FOR THE HOPELESS

My favorite book in the world states that hope deferred makes the heart sick. That is a compelling statement. Imagine a life without hope, without the belief that your current conditions would ever get better, that the life you are experiencing right now is the best that it would ever get. You don't even know where to start. Being so overwhelmed and consumed that you had very little fight left even to try to pursue a better life. As crazy as that sounds, that is the reality of millions and millions of people around the world. It has certainly been a reality that I have experienced and can definitely relate to. To live a life without hope is the equivalent of waving the white flag on your future. It's like a boxer going to his corner in the middle of a prize fight and asking his corner to throw in the towel. Despite all of the training, all the preparation, and all the countless hours in the gym, he has decided that the pressure from the opposition of his opponent is too much for him to continue. Once you lose hope, you have nothing else to fight for. Your current reality becomes the best you will ever experience. Belief and hope are the cornerstones of change. You have to fight for your dreams; you have to fight for your future. You have to fight to have the very best life that life has to offer. You deserve it! No one person is more deserving than you. Hope, Faith, and Belief are the fuel that ignites the fire needed to fight the good fight. Nothing in life comes easy, and anything worth having will require some fight and some sacrifice. It can get better. It will get better. But that does not come from simply hoping and wishing. Along with hope, there must be some action. Hope is the essential ingredient needed to fuel your decision to take action. Restore your hope, restore your faith, and know that all things are possible to him who believes!

THE AUDACITY OF HOPE

To achieve greatness, you must be audacious; you have to be so radical in your thinking that you have a total disregard for conventional wisdom. You have to be so confident in the possibility of you achieving your goals that you operate in a manner that suggests that conventional boundaries don't even apply to you. The thing about audacity is, it sees opportunities where other people see limitations. Audacity continually reminds us that there are no glass ceilings strong enough to withhold this force that lies inside of me. However, being audacious comes with a price. Many times, you will be misunderstood for having a dream so big that you are perceived as crazy. That's ok though. There is a saying that says that if people don't laugh at your dream, it's not big enough. When I think about audacity, I think about President Obama the 44th President of the United States of America. When did he first begin to believe that he could be the President of the United States? What gave him the audacity to believe that as an African American man, he could become the leader of the free world? A role that was historically reserved for rich white men from affluent backgrounds. Many people never even believed that we would see a black President in this lifetime. When you look at the systematic oppression of African Americans in this country since slavery, it was inconceivable that a man of color would ever hold such a prestigious position. Oh, but Mr. Obama had other plans, despite all of the opposition that was against him, he dared to believe that he could be something that nobody else even gave him a chance of becoming. And guess what, despite all of the opposition, all the hate and all the years of oppression, he shocked the world. What if he never dared to dream? What if he accepted the role that society deemed to be appropriate for him? You and I would have never witnessed history. There may be naysayers in your life right now saying you can't do that. How are you going to get that done? You don't have the resources to make that happen. Or maybe it's your own thoughts that have turned against you, the ones that speak fear and doubt so loud in your mind that it sounds like they are using a bullhorn. You have to be audacious enough to walk in the confidence that there is no limitation or opposition strong enough to hold you back.

YOU DESERVE IT

Contrary to what you believe to be true about yourself, there is nobody more deserving of the very best that life has to offer than you. You deserve to live a life full of the abundance that is out there for you. You deserve to live a life where your options are not limited due to lack of financial resources. The abundance of life is not just being financially secure; it's about experiencing the very best that life has to offer in your finances, in your relationships, in your relationship with your higher power as well as your health both physically and mentally. It's about being whole and knowing that you deserve wholeness in not just one area but all of these areas. If you are like most people, we experience success in some areas but struggle in others. Several people settle for less than what they really want because they internally struggle with believing that they are genuinely worthy of what they aspire to have or be. Trust me; you are not alone in this. Imagine me a young ghetto child from the inner-city streets born to a drug-addicted mother and absentee father aspiring to be a Motivational Speaker, Life Coach, and Author. What's the likelihood of that? What gives me the audacity to think that I could write a book with anything valuable to say that would help better the lives of others? I have no formal writing experience, I didn't complete college, and most of my experiences didn't prepare me for what I aspire to be. What makes me think that I'm the one for such a task as this? The better question is, what would make one think that I'm not the one for this? I know firsthand what it is to struggle with self-worth. I know what it is to doubt yourself and think you're not good enough. I know what it is to have a dream and vision so big that you refuse to let go of because, despite the odds of you fulfilling it, you are motivated by something on the inside that you just can't explain. I am the man for the job because despite dealing with some of the most difficult challenges that an individual can face, I have never given up. I have never let the pressures of what was coming against me be stronger than the hope that drove me from the inside. And this is not to toot my own horn at all. I'm merely using myself as an example of despite very meager beginnings and very little to be confident about; It is possible to find a way to persevere. I found a way to develop confidence and believe that not only was I worthy of what I wanted out of life, but also that I had what it took to bring my dreams to fruition. And guess what? You do too. You, my friend, deserve the very best of what life has to offer you. It's time to go and get it!

NOTHING IS IMPOSSIBLE

There is nothing that is impossible for them that believe. Keyword believe! You were created by the ALL knowing, the ALL powerful, the creator of the heavens and the earth. He who knows no lack, He who knows no failure. Do you not know that you are made in his image and his likeness? The very one that created this entire universe decided that you were important enough that he would create you. Do you think he would waste his time on creating a spirit and a soul which is an extension of him that would not be capable of accomplishing all that he set his or her mind to? You are fearfully and wonderfully made. You have genius inside you that you haven't even begun to tap into yet. There are parts of you that are so brilliant that if you ever start to tap into it, it would blow your mind. The human being is the greatest of all God's creation. When you even think about how he created us with such detail and intricacy, it is mind-blowing. The mind is an instrument capable of almost creating anything. Just for a moment, take a second to look around wherever you may find yourself right now. Everything that you are looking at right now originated in the mind of another human. From the telephone that you spend countless hours on daily, to the roads that you travel on to get to your various destinations, to the conversion of a tree to the paper that you are reading these words on right now, all originated in the mind of a human. You cannot tell me you are not powerful; you cannot tell me you are not brilliant, you cannot tell me that your mind does not possess the ability to bring forth something extraordinary. You are a genius in your own right. Your mind is the birthplace of amazing things. To access that ability, it starts with the belief that it exists within you, placed there by the divine. YOU ARE UNSTOPPABLE; YOU HAVE WHAT IT TAKES, YOU CAN ACHIEVE ANYTHING YOU PUT YOUR MIND TO! NOW GO OUT THERE AND DO IT!

THE POWER OF A MADE-UP MIND

There is nothing more powerful than a made-up mind. There is just something about when you make up your mind to do something that just starts to align things. It's like the universe just begins to respond to the demand that you place on it. There is something about when you declare I WILL NOT FAIL, I WILL NOT LOSE, I AM A WINNER, AND I WILL WIN AT ALL COST that you just begin to attract those things to you. A made-up mind is determined and resilient and will not give up at the first sign of difficulty or challenges. A made-up mind says that no matter what the cost I'm in this for the long haul. There is a quote that says that commitment is doing the thing that you said you were going to do long after the feeling you said it in is gone. Do you have that type of commitment to your dreams? Are you so invested in your future that you are ready to endure everything that goes along with it? The heartache, the pain, and the travail? Are you built for this? Do you have what it takes to stand tall in the face of adversity and refuse to be defeated? Because the truth of the matter is, that's what it's going to take. It's going to take you being like a prize fighter that refuses to go down. Although he has been battered and bruised for 12 rounds, there is something in him that refuses to go down. He is being punished with blow after blow, each one sending him to the canvas. But just like a robot he musters up the strength to pop right back up every time refusing to be defeated. Do you have that type of resolve in you? The answer to that question is YES. Whether you know it or not, you have that in you and more.

BETTER DAYS TO COME

If you have gained nothing else from this chapter, I hope that you have regained a sense of hope and faith that you can make the rest of your life the best of your life. The belief that you have a bright future ahead of you and that your later days shall be better than your former days. The possibilities are truly endless for you my friend. There is nothing that you are incapable of doing. Anything that you want you can have as long as you are willing to pay the price for it. All you have to do is simply believe and go after it. It's as simple as that. Will you have some good days? Yep! Will you have some bad ones? Absolutely! But the most important thing is that you press on. The process of becoming great is not an easy one. But it is one that is definitely worth it. You will have successes along the journey, you will also experience some failures, but it's ok, it's all part of the process. Each time you miss the mark, look at it as an opportunity to learn and use the information to make better-informed decisions the next time around. Your future is bright, your blessings are on the way, stay committed to the course, and you shall reap a reward if you faint not!

EXPANDING YOUR VISION OF YOURSELF

MAXIMUM EXPOSURE

As we dive into this next segment of this chapter, I want to talk to you about how important exposure is to your development and growth. It's hard to be more when you've never seen more or experienced more. In life, you only know what you know. Being exposed to new things can open up your mind to possibilities that you didn't even know existed. Exposure to the right people and environments can serve as the instruction manual on how to get to your goals. There is just something about being around grinders and go-getters that automatically makes you want more for yourself. It like being around the right people and makes you want to step your game up. It's like the energy is contagious. That's why it's always highly suggested that you find somebody that's already doing what you aspire to do well and align yourself with them. Mentors and coaches are huge. Even the best in their respective fields have coaches. There is something very valuable about having someone that can look at you objectively, assess your strengths and weaknesses, and push you to operate at your highest level. People that are already successful and have a unique perspective have already gone through the process of bumping their head figuring out what works and what doesn't work. They know from a mental, emotional and psychological standpoint what's required to experience success. Our journeys may not parallel theirs, but often they know fundamental principles that if applied could lead us down the road to success. Connecting yourself to the right person is very important, but what I have found to be true is that as soon as you begin to chase your dream passionately, the appropriate people start to appear and seek you out. Everybody wants to be associated with a winner, and as I said before, greatness attracts greatness. But there are still other things that you can do to position yourself to be in the right circles until the right people are ushered in your life. Networking is huge; there are so many ways to network living in the information age. You can go to seminars, conferences, professional and social mixers and the like to put yourself in environments where you will be around like-minded people. Social media and online communities are also huge venues to connect with the shakers and movers of this world. The goal is to connect yourself with people that build you up and offer you insight and wisdom that you can build upon. Be like a sponge soaking up everything that you can. Be a student, look to gain something from every individual that you encounter that you can put in a big melting pot of your own and put your own touch to. As you find yourself in these circles, always be conscientious of not appearing needy or like you don't belong there. The energy that you project can draw people closer to you or push people away from you. For some, this may be new to you, to others, this may be a rodeo that you have attended several times. But no matter where you find yourself in life, it is essential to continue to grow and evolve. The most important thing to remember is that the more information that you have, the better you are positioned to apply what you know. Knowledge and wisdom are usually gained through our experiences.

KNOWLEDGE WITHOUT COLLEGE

Although exposure is essential to your success, the amount of info that you possess is paramount to you being successful. Think about it, what's the difference between the wealthy and the poor? It's the amount of information that they possess. They say that most people that come into a sudden fortune are usually broke within five years of receiving it. While the opposite is true for people that have amassed a fortune by taking very intentional and deliberate steps to become successful. They say that most millionaires can lose it all and get it back again. Why? It's because they know exactly what it takes to be a millionaire. They may not have every detail on what the course will be, but they know the fundamental principles that are required to become successful. Being that it is a place that they have been before, it's not as hard to get back there the second time because they have figured out the blueprint. Whether they figured out the blueprint through trial and error or were given an instructional manual, the information was the game changer. Think of it in this way, if you were traveling across the country to a place you had never been, and I verbally told you how to get there, you would stand very little chance at arriving at your destination. But if I gave you a map with all the information that you needed to make it to your exact location, it would significantly increase your chances of arriving at your destination. Knowledge and information are the maps required to navigate the roads of success. What most people don't realize is that learning and acquiring information are not exclusive to traditional school. We live in a day and age where anything that you want to learn is at your fingertips. With Google and YouTube, there is no excuse not to learn how to do anything that you want to do. Being a lifelong learner is important. Reading and studying the minds of the great thinkers of the world can provide you with insight that can change your entire life. It's important to feed yourself constantly with information that will build you up and empower you to heighten your thinking. As your thinking grows, so will your life. It doesn't matter how you consume the information; the important thing is that you do. Reading, audiobooks, YouTube, and the internet are all good sources of information. The more knowledge that you have puts you in a better position to execute upon which you know.

PREPARING YOUR GIFT

Many people want to start at the point of excellence. They want to start their careers with their gifts fully mature and developed. Many people look at the lives of those that are successful and don't realize what it took to get there. There is a saying that it takes 10,000 hours of practicing a thing to get to the level of mastery. What many don't see is the behind the scenes preparation that it took to get to a point where they could operate at a high level in their gift. By the time we actually get to see the great skill set on display, there have been countless hours of grueling repetition spent perfecting their craft. Now don't get me wrong, some people are just naturally gifted with a particular talent, but being gifted and being great are two different things. Being gifted is natural abilities that you were instinctively born with, greatness is the intentional act of developing that gift. This revelation began to sink in for me as my son was going into his senior football season in high school. As I started to think about what I needed to do to prepare my son for the next level, I realized that talent by itself wasn't good enough anymore. It may have been good enough on the level he was on, but not for the next level. I told him the same thing that I tell many of the athletes that I work with, which is that your competition is not the guys that you are playing against, but it's guys your age all across the nation. Because that's who you will be competing with for those college scholarships. So, while preparing for your current competition is important, your level of play needs to be consistent with the level that you aspire to play on, which is a whole other level. Scouts don't come out and evaluate you simply on what you can do at this level; they assess you on the potential that you have to play on the next level. So that means that you need to practice, study, and prepare differently if you want what you say you want, which is to go to the next level. So, armed with this information, I did what any football Dad would do; I went out and got the best trainer I could for him. A guy by the name of Jamal Liggins.

He has trained the likes of Marshawn Lynch, Odell Beckham Jr., Josh Johnson, and Reggie Bush just to name a few. I mean the guy's resume is impressive. So, what did my son do with this million-dollar opportunity? He took it for granted. He would go to training unprepared, malnourished, sluggish, and just performing poorly. So eventually, I stopped investing in someone that wasn't invested in himself. So that particular season he ended up redshirting his first year of junior college. But something happened between that first year and that second year of college. The coach switched his position. In high school he played running back, he was a smaller, speedy, shifty type back. But at the college level, they wanted to move him to slot receiver, a position that he had never played before. So, unlike before, he was no longer playing a position that he had played since he was ten years old. So, the confidence that was associated with the familiarity of playing a position that he excelled at all of his life was gone. So now he had to work to develop a skill set at this new position which stretched him. That may have been one of the best things that ever happened to him because it forced him to dig down deep and work. I knew that his work ethic had caught up with his talent when I called him one day and said, "What are you doing?" He said, "I'm running routes let me call you back," I said, "It's raining." He replied, "I know I'm running routes have to call you back." At that point, I knew that he had finally begun to understand that the gift by itself is not good enough. What you do with the gift is everything. There is a saying that hard work beats talent when talent doesn't work hard. What are you doing to prepare the gift that God gave you? Your gift is only as good as what you do with it!

REDEFINING YOUR BOUNDARIES

In order to overcome the limitations that have been set in your mind, you must retrain your mind to believe what is true about you. You have to believe that you are gifted, that you are talented and fully capable of anything that you set your mind to. I can hear some of you now saying that it is very cliché and basic. How can I change my mind by simply changing the way that I think?

You would be amazed at what positive thinking can do. It's not the thinking that will change your life, but the action that you will begin to take once you believe that you are capable of doing what you desire. To think differently, you must start by examining and taking accountability for what is allowed to go into your mind. The quality of your mind determines the course of your life, so it would only make sense that you would want to evaluate what is allowed to go into your mind. As I mentioned earlier, many of us have many years of negative messaging which I liken to viruses on the hard drives of our mind. In order to erase the mind viruses of the lies that we have accepted about ourselves, we have to acknowledge first that they are there and then decide to take some action to rid them from our lives permanently. I would like to suggest a 3-step process to overcome self-imposed limitations that I have used in my own life.

1. **Rid It (Rid Your Mind Of Limiting Beliefs)**- In order to begin to rid your mind of limiting beliefs, the first step is to acknowledge that they exist and have been standing in between you and your dreams. Once you accept that the beliefs have been limiting you, it's important to try to identify where these beliefs originated from. Where did you first begin to doubt yourself? When did you start to believe that you couldn't have the life that you wanted? This process of transparency and self-discovery will be a hard one, and it will force you to take ownership of the self-sabotaging thinking that you have allowed to define your boundaries. This process may take some time, and you may have to revisit the process several times, but it is essential to you reprogramming your mind that you acknowledge the problem and find the origins of it to begin the process of addressing it, which is exactly what I did. Years ago, I started to do the work of tracing the origins of my self-imposed limitations back to being denied by my father as a child. As you can imagine, seeing your father in the lives of your brothers and sisters and claiming them was hard to process as a young child. It made me feel like

what's wrong with me? At the time, I was too young to process what was happening, but the rejection that I was experiencing caused me to doubt myself. It affected my self-esteem as well as my self-worth without me even being aware of it. I felt a lot of awkwardness, shame, and isolation and I just thought this is the way that I was. It wasn't until I went back and did the work to understand how I came to be the way that I was that I realized the origin. There have been other events that have also contributed to me feeling like that; so with all of them compounded together, they really did a number on me. The work of going back and addressing the root cause of my self-imposed limitations puts me in a position to be able to overcome them. Although the work was hard, I'm glad that I began the process because there is no way to overcome the things that you don't address. Many adults behave in ways that are a direct result of things that they experienced as children and until the work is done to find the root causes of their issues, it will be impossible to overcome them. Look at it like this; when landscapers find weeds in your garden, and they want to get rid of them, what do they do? They dig the weeds up by the root because if you just try to cut them down without digging up the roots, the weeds will continue to pop up choking the life out of everything good in the garden. The same thing rings true in our lives; until we begin to start cutting our issues down by the root, they will continue to keep popping up in our lives. It may be time for some of us to start cutting our weeds down by the roots so that our gardens can flourish.

2. **Fill It (Condition Your Mind For Success)**- To rid your mind of self-defeating thoughts, it is important to replace those thoughts with new ones. The quality of your mind is mainly dependent on what you feed your mind. The mind is just like the body, in that it needs nourishment to thrive and operate at its fullest potential. The best way to interrupt some of the self-defeating thoughts that may be

holding you back is to feed your mind constantly with information that will expand your boundaries and your vision of yourself. You control your mind and what's inputted into it daily. The mind is a funny thing because it's susceptible to empowering thoughts and information in the same way it is subject to self-defeating thoughts. The only person that has the authority to control what's entered is you. I believe that people have much more control over their mind than they give themselves credit for. You have to direct your mind in the way in which you want it to go. So make it a point every day to spend some time conditioning your mind for success.

3. **Protect It (Protect Your Mind From Negative Thoughts And Influences**)- Your mind is your absolute biggest resource. Your mind is the vehicle that will take you through this life. So, it would only make sense that you make efforts to protect it. Think about it. What do we do with the things that are valuable to us? We lock them up and keep them protected from thieves so that they can't come in and steal from us. Well, guess what? Self-doubt and self-imposed limitations are thieves looking to steal your confidence and your belief that you have what it takes to be successful at whatever it is that you aspire to do. Always protect your mind and guard it as if you were guarding Fort Knox because your mind is the most valuable asset that you have. You have to be intentional about the environments that your mind can be influenced in, the conversations that you allow yourself to engage in and the people that you give access to you. You are valuable; your mind is valuable, so protect it as if you know its value!

THE DECLARATION

The lies that we have previously accepted about our limitations have crippled us. But today that stops! I declare from this day forward that we will walk in a newness, knowing that the only boundaries that truly exist for us are the ones that we allow to reside in our minds. Going forward, we will go about everything that we do with the audacity to believe that it is impossible for us to fail. We will walk in the self-assured confidence that we are fully capable of doing great things. We will always remain cognizant that we deserve the very best that life has to offer. And we will redefine our boundaries to reflect the life that we want to live. We are victorious!

CHAPTER 4
YOUR FEELINGS DON'T MATTER

"Your feelings are an unreliable compass. Never let your feelings inform what you do because after the feelings have subsided clarity makes an appearance."

—Edward L. Moore

The journey to success is a very emotional one. When you are going after a dream or goal that is beyond you, you will experience a wide range of emotions as you pursue your dreams. Sometimes you will be excited, and things will be clicking on all cylinders and other times you may feel down and depressed questioning if you will ever get to your goals. This rollercoaster of emotions is normal and is as much a part of the journey as developing a plan to pursue your goals. But what you must remember as you experience bouts of doubt, frustration, and fear is that emotions are merely emotions. Just because you feel a certain way does not mean that it is rooted in truth. Emotions are an unreliable compass. Many people perceive how they feel to be an absolute truth and that is simply not true. Just because you feel something is true does not mean that it is true. Think about it, how many times have you been convinced that something that you thought to be true was true just because you felt it was that turned out to be untrue? Right now, this very second, you may be thinking that your current situation is the best it will get, or that you will never arrive at your goal or dream, or that there are just too many odds against you. I'm here to tell you that just because you feel that way doesn't make it true. People place too much value on feelings. They let their feelings dictate their entire lives. It's unwise to trust your feelings as they change all the time. We have to gain control of our feelings, or our feelings will control us. At the very least we must at least be able to put our feelings in the proper perspective to know that just because I feel a certain way doesn't necessarily make it true. Emotions can have a huge impact on our lives, and if they are not constantly measured against the truth, they can lead us to make decisions that are not in our best interest because of how we perceive things to be.

EMOTIONAL SLAVES

One of the things that people don't realize is the HUGE role that emotions play in our lives. One of the main reasons that emotions play such a huge role in our lives is because most people's perception is their reality. For most people, what they perceive to be true becomes the gospel for them. That is a very dangerous way to move through life because your perception is based on how you feel and not on facts. There will be some times where your feelings will line up with the facts sure. But what about when those instances when they don't? Many people make decisions based on what they feel only to find out later that what they felt wasn't true. Or even worse make decisions that were not in their best interest, because when your emotions are high, rarely do we make the soundest decisions. This is why it is always suggested not to make decisions when you are upset or angry because when emotions are high rationale goes out of the window. Your emotions can become an enemy of your destiny if left unchecked. Your emotions can literally work against you. We all have seen the individual that lashes out due to anger and makes a stupid decision that they later end up regretting. You have to be careful of what emotions you allow to creep in on you and always examine what you are feeling. Unchecked emotions can be crippling and can stand in the way of you and your dreams. Fear especially can be crippling. There are millions of people that have never decided to go after their dreams because of the fear of not achieving their dream or how people may perceive them. It's like the singer that has everything it takes to be a superstar, they have the look, they have the talent and a voice that would blow your socks off, but they stay hidden behind the curtain of life because of the perceived fear of not being good enough. Your emotions have a bigger impact on you than you may think. Think about the last time you were really angry or upset. Did you feel like you were in the best state to be productive? Were your thoughts clear? Did you feel like you were able to perform at optimal levels? Even as I sit here now, and I think about my personal experience with unregulated emotions, I'm reminded of all the times that they stood in the way of me getting where I wanted to be in life. Whether it was the anger that always encouraged me to make impulsive, irrational decisions or the fear and self-doubt that had me living beneath my privilege because I questioned if I was good enough or the depression that I battled with that made it a struggle to get out of bed.

When I talk about the struggle to maintain healthy emotions, I don't talk about it from a theoretical standpoint; I talk about it from lived experience. I have seen firsthand how not regulating my emotions has left me stuck on the treadmill of life going nowhere fast. So many people let their feelings be the reason that they don't live out their potential. While your feelings are a part of you and the lens in which you see the world through, the thing that I want you to realize is as it relates to you getting where you want to go in life is that THEY DO NOT MATTER! Your feelings are just feelings, they are not necessarily real, and they do not have to hold you back. What you perceive is not absolute truth. You may be scared, so what, do it scared! You may be confused, seek out clarity. You may not feel motivated, motivate yourself! Whatever you do, just don't let your emotions be the obstacle that stands between you and destiny. There will be days when you don't feel motivated. There will be days when you may feel down; there will also be days when you question if you will actually arrive at your goal. The important thing to understand is that they are merely feelings. The task before you is still at hand and the only way that it will be accomplished is through your blood, sweat, and tears. So, despite the wide range of emotions that you will experience along the journey, you still have to find a way to win in the face of those emotions. We have to be bigger than what we feel.

ASSESSING YOUR EMOTIONAL HEALTH

If you were to examine the role that emotions currently play in your life, would it be safe to say that you are emotionally healthy? Are you able to manage your emotions in such a way that you can make sound decisions despite what comes at you? Are you able to break through negative feelings when they arise and still carry out your objectives and goals despite how you feel? These are some questions that I would like you to examine as you assess your emotional health. The thing about being emotionally healthy is that we can be healthy in some areas and be in need of an emotional overhaul in others. Working to maintain emotional health is an ongoing process that we must stay engaged in for the rest of our lives if we want to remain emotionally healthy. In what areas of your life do you need to work on emotionally? I know for me it has always been easier for me to manage professional relationships and relationships with people that are not close to me. There is just something about relationships with people that are close to me that have been more challenging. Those close to your heart naturally can affect you in ways that others can't because there is a relationship there, there is emotion there. And so for me, I have had to be more conscientious of how I respond to emotionally charged situations with people that are close to me. What are the areas that you need to pay special attention to? For you, it may be something entirely different, but everybody has certain emotional triggers that they are more susceptible to. So, when you work on being emotionally healthy or as many describe it as being emotionally intelligent, you have to do a self-assessment on yourself by asking yourself these kinds of questions. Because if unchecked these same emotions can wreak havoc in your life.

Your emotional health is priceless, and if you have gotten to a point where you are emotionally healthy, trust me you have paid a price for it. You probably have been through a wide range of things and have had to make healthy decisions despite how you felt at the moment. That's something to be commended, that's also something to be protected. When you get to a place of emotional peace, how can you protect that? What strategies can you put in place to make sure that you do everything within your power to stay emotionally balanced? Some may think it's tedious to plan and strategize in advance but trust me it works. I was just talking to a colleague of mine today, and he was telling me about how the police came to his house with a warrant for him because of something his son did in his car. Mind you we are both Life Coaches for the City of Oakland. Because the son did not admit to the offense, his car was impounded, and it will cost him $1500.00 to get it out. My first question to him was, how did you respond to your son when this happened? His response was EPIC! He said, "I'm glad that I was not at home when they came because it gave me time to process the situation. Had I been home, I may have responded in anger, but because I had a long drive home, it gave me time to process the situation." He continued, "I went on a roller coaster of emotions as it relates to the situation. At times I was very angry to the point of aggression, but at other points, a cooler head prevailed." Ultimately the cooler head prevailed, and he was able to make the decision that was in the best interest of all those involved because of being intentional about his decision despite how he felt. Imagine preparing responses to situations that you know you will inevitably face in advance. In no way, shape, form or fashion am I suggesting that this is a full proof plan to respond correctly, but what I am suggesting is that if you prepare for emotional challenges that you face in advance, you may stand a better chance to overcome them. So as you prepare to become the best version of yourself emotionally, the more you can do to prepare to respond to the trials and tribulations of life, the better you position yourself to respond to them accordingly.

DON'T BE DETOURED

If I could be all the way transparent to you at this very moment, and I would even go back as far as the past few months, I have been going through hell emotionally. All kinds of things have been coming at me from every angle. I mean all kinds of things. I have felt extremely overwhelmed, I have been tired and just downright worn out. I have struggled to overcome feelings of doubt and I have had things happen to me that have made me feel like giving up. But guess what? I DIDN'T! I am still in the fight! Nobody promised that life would be easy. Sometimes it will be extremely hard, but you much like me only have two choices which are to dig down deep or give up! And if you are reading this book, it is my hunch that you do not want to give up. And I am with you! We are in this thing together. Soldiers on the same battlefield. I'm telling you that nobody is immune to the trials and tribulations of life, but we can make it. We have to. Life is interesting; it's like when I started writing this chapter all hell broke out in my life. It was like life was challenging me to see if I really embodied what I promote or if it was just talk. There are not many self-help experts that would be this transparent with you because of the notion that we need to have it all together. We need to have all of the answers and never struggle with anything. But my belief is different; nobody has it all together! But what you can have is a toolbelt full of tools that you can access when you experience negative emotions that could come in between you and your destiny. I'm so very thankful for the tools and information that I have in my toolbelt that has allowed me to persevere in some of the most challenging times in my life.

I believe the fact that despite everything that I have been going through and still found a way to push forward to even write these very words that you are reading speaks more loudly and inspires more hope than me pretending like I have everything together. I could very well act like I face no challenges and as a result, can provide you with steps so that you can make your life perfect like mine. Of course, I'm facetious, but that's not realistic, that is not how life works. You have to fight; you have to be a fighter! And you have to fight with a mind that's centered on truth. The truth is just because things feel a certain way doesn't mean that it will always be that way. I had to fight through the feelings that have been overwhelming me this very week. Thank God for truth and the understanding that although I go through times like this, that I have to keep my eyes on the prize. No matter what you are going through, you do not have to be detoured from your goals in life. We must get what we came for! There is no way around it. As I mentioned earlier in this chapter, you must be an overcomer of your emotions or they will be an overcomer of you. In order to overcome them, you must recognize the power that emotions have. You have to keep it real to yourself and assess how your emotions impact you. The very first step in overcoming negative emotions is to really be honest about how they affect you. Over the course of this past week, I had to be honest with myself that the emotions that I was feeling had become so heavy that they were impacting several areas in my life. They affected my work, impacted how I responded to my children, and even my desire for the things that I regularly do that make my life better. As I came to that realization that the emotions that I was feeling were impacting my life in such great way, I had to make a decision to process through what I was feeling and allow the truth to permeate my mind. And as I calmed down, I was able to see more avenues that I could take to address my challenges. When those negative feelings arise, you have to recognize them for what they are, just feelings. You have to find a way to take everything that you are feeling and figure out how to use it and make it work for you. Take all of the fear, all of the worry, all of the anxiety and face it head on and use it as the fuel by which you overcome. It's almost like you have to get mad at the opposition that has tried to come against you, which has tried to steal your hope and use that same energy to go even harder. It is imperative that you stay in continual assessment of your feelings so that you can make decisions that are in your best interest despite how you feel in any situation.

In this chapter, we have discussed how significant of a role that emotions play in our lives and how important it is to keep them in perspective. The overarching theme of this entire chapter is very simple. Do not let negative emotions detour you from achieving your goals. There will always be times when your feelings will be counterproductive to what you aspire to achieve, but you must press on anyway. Never allow what you feel to become more important than what you know you must do. Feelings come and go, but opportunities don't always last forever! Learn how to persevere even when you don't feel like it, and trust me there will be many days when you don't feel like it. That's the difference between those that are successful and those that are not. Those that are successful feel the same things that everybody else feels, they just find a way to press through it. They work hard on mastering their feelings and not letting their feelings master them. And they also work on maintaining emotional health because they understand just how detrimental emotional health is to their success. How you deal with your feelings will ultimately determine how far you will go in life. What a shame it would be if you didn't make it to your God-ordained destiny because of some feelings that will probably have changed by the time you realize how insignificant they were about achieving your goals.

PART TWO
ACCOUNTABILITY

CHAPTER 5
TIME IS RUNNING OUT

"Those who make the worst use of their time are the first to complain of its brevity."

—JEAN DE LA BRUYERE

T**ime is one** of, if not the most valuable, commodities that we have in this life. Think about it even your most prized possessions can be replaced. And if you have enough money you can buy just about anything that you want to. But one thing that you can never purchase or manipulate is time. Each man is allotted a certain amount of time on this earth, and after it's gone, there is no replacing it. Interestingly enough, a lot of people go through life squandering it as if it holds no real value. It's one of those things that you don't miss until it's gone. If you were to ask somebody on the cusp of transitioning into eternity if they could have a little more of anything they would undoubtedly tell you more time. What are you doing with your time? How effective have you been in utilizing your time to your benefit thus far in your life? We only get one go around at this thing called life, so it's essential to use every second that we have on the clock to maximize the time given to us.

WE THINK THAT WE ALWAYS HAVE TIME

You see, one of the biggest problems that we face is that we think that we will always have time to do the things that we need to do later. And we keep putting off what needs to be done to a time that we never get around to. We always put off things until that magical day "someday" and before we know it, a lot of time has elapsed and someday never comes. You will not always be on this earth, and no man knows the day or hour when his number will be called. So with that being said, it's important that we use the time that we have wisely. One of the things that always keep things in perspective for me is the understanding that I could have more days behind me than in front of me. That's a startling realization, but it keeps me grounded and appreciative of the time that I have left here on this planet. Tomorrow is not promised to you my friend and your goals will not fulfill themselves. In the words of the superstar hip-hop group Outkast, you have to get up get out and get something. Don't wait to do later what you could be doing now and continue to prolong your destiny. I'm sure you have 1,000 legitimate reasons why right now is not the right time for you to be doing the things that you should be doing, and I empathize with you. But let's keep it real, an excuse is still just an excuse all day long. And if you haven't noticed, the name of this book is, "No Excuses When Failure Is No Longer An Option." There are a million-other people that face the same challenges that you do, that have the same schedule that you do that find a way to get it done anyway. Imagine getting to the end of your days in the 4th quarter of life with very few seconds on the clock as you face transitioning over into eternity regretful of not using the time that you had allotted on this earth wisely. What a tragedy!

WINDOW OF OPPORTUNITY

My favorite motivational speaker in the world, Eric Thomas, often talks about maximizing the opportunity of a lifetime in the lifetime of the opportunity. What many people don't realize is that there is a window of opportunity associated with some dreams. You have a window of time to maximize the opportunity, and when that window is up, the opportunity is gone with it as well, and you can never get it back. You may get another opportunity at something else, but that particular opportunity is gone. Let me give you an example from my personal life. When I was in high school, I was a two-sport athlete; I played both basketball and football. I was really athletic and had been since I was a small child, so I was always engaged in some sports. So naturally, when I got to high school I joined the football and basketball team. I was good in both but may have been just a little more advanced in basketball because I played more coming up. But the more I began to play football I fell in love with it. What I eventually ended up finding out is that I was pretty good at it. I played running back and outside linebacker. Anybody that knows anything about football knows that those are some pretty celebrated positions. But at any rate my freshman and sophomore year I dominated in both sports. But as I begun to get involved more with the wrong crowd and started to focus less and less on my academics, it got to the point to where I didn't have the grades to play as I was transitioning from junior varsity to varsity. I was a sure shot for the starting varsity running back position, but without the grades, I wasn't able to play. And the next year was the same thing. What a wasted opportunity. It's an utter shame that I never got to touch the field as a varsity player. Varsity is where it really counts. That's where scouts come to look for players to recruit to offer scholarships to play at their universities. Who knows how far I could have made it? We will never know because you are only eligible to play four years of sports in high school and after those four years was up that window of opportunity was gone and so was that dream with it. Had I known what I know now, I would've been more mindful of the time that I had to make that dream come true. That window of opportunity to play ball at the next level started to close on me, and it came a lot quicker than I expected. It always happens like that; the window closes a lot faster than we anticipate it to close. Four years seems like a long time when you're a freshman but before you know it, two years have gone by, and you're a junior headed into your senior year. And if you're not intentional about maximizing every second, every minute, and every hour of every day, you will end up with regretting not fulfilling the opportunity that was before you to live out your dream. What areas of your life have you let the window of opportunity close on you? What are some of the goals that you had that were attached to a timeline that you didn't fulfill? Most people feel as if "Oh I'll have another chance to address it tomorrow," and before long, tomorrow turns into another day and then that day turns into a month, that month turns into a year, and before you know it, that dream has become a faint memory. When you have something before you, do it swiftly, don't let the window of opportunity close on you, and understand that some dreams have an expiration date, so it's important to make the most of every opportunity.

TIME JUST KEEPS ON SLIPPING

WHEN THE WINDOW CLOSES

When you allow the window of opportunity to expire on your goal or your dreams, you miss out on opportunities that you will never get back. The time span in which you could maximize on that opportunity has elapsed and as bad as you may want to get it back it is over. What I wouldn't give to have my varsity years back to make an impact in football. Just to see what I could have become if I put my all into my dream of becoming a professional football player. I have had to live with the reality that I will never know what I could have become had I capitalized on that opportunity. And to be truthful, that's a bitter pill to swallow. I have since reinvented myself and found something that I am just as passionate about, but no matter how you slice it, that dream of playing professional football is gone. That was a very costly life lesson. One that I often share with others in hopes that it will inspire them not to take the opportunity that they have in front of them for granted. Capitalizing on opportunities is paramount to success. Nobody wants to live a life regretting the opportunities that they allowed to slip through their hands.

AT A STAND STILL

When we don't capitalize on the opportunities that are before us, we stay stuck in place never making any real progress. We stay stuck at a standstill on the treadmill of life until we can figure out the next venture to pursue. The dangerous thing about that is that it can take years to reinvent yourself and find another dream to pursue. Some people sink into a depression and never even attempt to find something that they are passionate about outside of their initial dream. I mean we have all heard the stories of the person that had a dream, and once it became apparent that they were not going to be able to live out their dream, they faded into oblivion frustrated and confused about what to do next. Some even become so jaded and mad that life didn't hand them what they wanted that they retreated to a corner and never tried to do anything else. That's why it's so important to take action in the lifetime of the opportunity to avoid the consequences of squandering time and stagnation is one of them.

WHAT'S THE IMPACT?

The decisions you make impact everybody around you whether you know it or not. The choices that you make impact everybody connected to you whether bad or good. If you make positive decisions, those in your life will benefit from the positive decisions that you make, and if you make negative decisions, those in your life will inherit the consequences of those negative decisions. I would even venture to say that the people that are connected to you are equally impacted by the decisions that you don't make. When you don't operate in your highest self, you will not experience the rewards that come from operating in such a manner. And as a result, those in your life will not experience the quality of life that they could have had if you operated in your highest self. If you struggle, they will struggle; if by persistence and self-discipline you reach your goals, those connected to you will reap the rewards as well. I had no idea that when I was waddling through life as a young man making poor decision after poor decision that the decisions that I was making would affect my future children. They inherited my struggle because of poor decisions that I made 20 years before that. I wish somebody had told me that when I was cutting class that years later, it would not only affect me but the people that I loved the most. I encourage you today to play the tape forward and to consider how your persistence or your apathy will affect those connected to you and make a decision today that would create a better tomorrow.

WHAT HAPPENED TO THE TIME?

I want you to take a few moments to ponder the questions that I am about to ask you. I want you to think about these questions and be honest with yourself. What opportunities have you let slip through the cracks of your hands? What are some of the goals that you had identified that you wanted to achieve that you were not able to bring to fruition because you did not do it in the lifetime of the opportunity? How did that feel for you to know that the opportunity was there but because of your inability to capitalize when the opportunity was before you, you missed out on that opportunity forever? A more important question is, are you willing to let the same cycle repeat itself? Good opportunities don't come around always, so when they do, we have to be prepared to capitalize on them promptly.

REGAINING YOUR TIME

TAKE A LOOK AT WHAT'S BEEN HOLDING YOU BACK

One of the first steps to overcome any problem or issue in your life is to do some introspective work and look at what was causing the problem in the first place. What was going on with you that caused you to procrastinate and not seize the opportunities that were before you? Was it that you were distracted? Did you secretly doubt that you could achieve your goal? Or were you just not prepared when the opportunity presented itself? Whatever the reason you must be honest with yourself about what it was, so the next time you have an opportunity, what held you back previously won't hold you back again. What I have found to be true about dream chasing or pursuing goals is that it takes a huge amount of self-discipline and intestinal fortitude. A lot of what holds people back is internal barriers. Once I got to a place where I was honest about the things that were hindering me internally and started to address them, I then was able to start seeing some progress because I went to the root cause of the problem. Many people try to achieve goals and set up these beautiful, elaborate plans but fall short many times because they never took the time to address what was holding them back. It's like putting a band-aid on a bullet wound when we don't address the underlying issue that's been holding you back. Once you address the issue, then and only then will you be in a position to maximize the opportunity of a lifetime in the lifetime of an opportunity.

PREPARE FOR THE OPPORTUNITY BEFORE IT PRESENTS ITSELF

There is a saying that says that it's better to be prepared for an opportunity and not have one than to have one and not be prepared. It's important to prepare for an opportunity long before it presents itself. That's like an athlete that hasn't spent countless hours working out in the gym and preparing their body to compete at a high level getting an opportunity to play professional sports, how do you think they would fare? Do you think that they would be able to compete with all the other athletes that had been preparing for the opportunity? The same is true in just about any area of life, when you are not prepared, when the opportunity comes, chances are you won't execute well. You end up providing an underdeveloped product that could actually do more harm to your reputation than good. When we are unprepared, we end up squandering the very things that we say we want. It's one thing to say that you want something and a whole other to do the things to have what it is that you say that you want. Preparation is essential to executing well when doing anything. I can usually tell the likelihood of someone succeeding at something by the amount of investment they put into preparing for their goal. I have a client that I am coaching that I knew would accomplish his goal just by the amount of time that he put into preparing for his opportunity. I saw this young man dedicate countless hours of study and commitment to pursuing his goal so that when the time came for him to execute, he was able to do so. His first two attempts at a test he was taking, he failed by just a few questions, but on his third attempt, he succeeded because not only was he persistent, but he also had prepared for the opportunity.

CONDITION YOURSELF TO ACT IN A TIMELY MANNER

If you want to be an executor, it is critical that you act promptly. Most people spend more time sitting around plotting and strategizing what they want to do than they do in pursuing it. You have to act! Even if you don't know everything to do, do something. If you sit around waiting for the coast to be clear and the conditions to be right, you will be waiting forever. You must act NOW! What's something that you have been saying that you want to do that you have not acted upon? I'm going to encourage you, in the same way, one of my good friends encouraged me. I had been talking about becoming a motivational speaker for seven years, one day on the phone, he said, "Man you've been talking about becoming a speaker for a long time, when are you actually going to start?" That was a startling reality that hit me like a ton of bricks. I said, "You know what, I am going to do something this week." And as a result of that conversation, I ended up starting a weekly YouTube show that I do called "Motivational Mondayz." The first show was horrible; I was sitting in my living room recording on a cell phone looking and sounding awkward as I tried to deliver a message. But guess what? That first video despite how bad it was, was the birth of my career as a speaker. I can't tell you how many other great things have happened since starting with that initial decision to act. This book that you are reading right now is a product of that initial decision. Not to mention the speaking engagements, the life coaching opportunities, the merchandise and just the opportunity to live out my dream. There is nothing in the world that I would rather be doing than what I am doing right now. And you can do the same thing; your dream is there waiting for you to simply act upon it.

SET A GOAL DATE WITH BENCHMARKS ALONG THE WAY

As you begin to move promptly and capitalize on your opportunities, it's important to set up accountability measures to help you stay on course to complete your tasks promptly. One of the things that have worked for me is having an accountability partner. My accountability partner is someone that I admire and have a great deal of respect for. He also holds me accountable for what I say I'm going to do. He actually agreed to be my partner to help me complete this book. I knew myself, and I knew that if I was going to finish this book promptly, I needed to set up an accountability measure to hold me accountable. That is one of the best decisions that I have ever made. Since starting to write the book, I have written more than I have ever written before working with him in a short amount of time. It has motivated me to know that every other Sunday, he will be contacting me to see if I completed a chapter. Having that accountability measure in place pushes me where I would usually say, you know what, I'll take a day off, or I'll get to it later. I respect him, and I appreciate his time, and I value his support, so I do everything within my power to have those chapters in on time. Have I been perfect every time? No, but for the most part having an accountability partner has pushed me toward my goal much faster than I would've gotten there on my own. This I am sure of. It is also important to have checks and balances and benchmarks to have along the way with a timeline. The very first thing that my accountability partner had me do was outline the entire book by chapters and create a timeline for when each chapter would be completed. He then went a step further by asking me to identify when the book would be going to editing and then print. Every time a deadline comes, he checks in with me to see where I am in the process. I can't tell you how helpful having an accountability measure in place has been. My question to you is, what would it look like for you to put accountability measures in place to do what you say you want to do? Do you have anybody in your life that you respect enough to hold you accountable for your goals and aspirations? I strongly encourage you to set up an accountability measure if you are serious about your goals.

The most important thing is to realize that opportunities don't last always. There is a window of opportunity associated with most dreams, and when it's gone, it's gone forever. We have to act promptly with every opportunity because if we don't, we may end up repeating the same cycle of regretting the opportunities that we didn't take advantage of. Tomorrow is promised to no man, all we have is today and what we do with it is paramount to achieving success. We have to be intentional with every second of every day to maximize our effectiveness to achieve greatness. I hope that this chapter has motivated you to do some reflective work to look at what has held you back in the past and develop a plan on how to address it going forward. The accountability measures that you put in place serve as very useful tools to stay on track. It's easier to get to a goal when you have someone to be accountable to with timelines and benchmarks set in place. I hope that you will never let another opportunity pass by you because you are ill prepared and don't efficiently use your time. I can say with all confidence that if you are reading this book, you are looking to address the barriers in your life that have been holding you back. I support you one thousand percent. It is one of the most liberating experiences in the world when you do the deep internal work that frees you from the chains and anchors that keep us from excelling. But I promise you that when you go to the root cause and address the source of your procrastination, you will soar to heights that you have never imagined.

CHAPTER 6
DREAM KILLERS

Most of the dreams that have suffered to death were murdered by their own owners.

—Israelmore Ayivor

Whenever you begin to pursue your dreams or attempt to do anything of significance, there will always be things that threaten to hinder you from getting to your goals. Everywhere you look, there will be distractions and temptations constantly fighting for your attention and your focus, with the goal of getting you off track. There will also be things that will try to draw you away from what you need to be doing to be successful every second of every day. Those things that I am referring to are called dream killers. Very simply put, dream killers are anything that has the potential to stop you from getting to your dreams. In this chapter, I would like to discuss two different types of dream killers. The first is the internal dream killers or things on the inside of us that threaten our dreams. And the second is the external dream killers or things on the outside of us that equally pose a threat to the life of our dreams. Let's start off by looking at the two most prominent internal dream killers that usually impact people's ability to bring their dreams to fruition. The first dream killer that I would like to examine is the dream killer of distraction.

DISTRACTION

THE ENEMY OF DISTRACTION

Never in all of history has there been so many things vying for our attention. With the emergence of technology, (social media, television, and tabloids) it's easy to spend a whole day consumed in entertainment. These practices have become so ingrained in our culture that it has become the norm. Think about it. What's one of the first things that you do in the morning when you wake up? I'm sure if you are like the average person, grabbing for your phone is one of the first things that you do even before you have fully awakened and gotten out of bed. In any major city in the world, you can find people aimlessly walking down the street so consumed in their telephones that their safety takes a back seat to updating their statuses and uploading their selfies. Things have changed considerably within the last decade, even children have become so inundated with technology that they don't even engage in regular activities anymore. When I was a kid, we got excited about going outside, riding bikes, and engaging in physical activities like playing basketball or football. Nowadays, if you give a child the option to go outside and play vs. playing with one of their many electronic devices, you would be hard-pressed to pry them away from their gadgets.

Don't get me wrong, technology has made life a lot easier and made things more readily accessible to us, but that didn't entirely come without a cost. The average American spends a considerable amount of time on social media each day. There is a study that suggests that social networkers between the ages of 18-34 spend an average 3.8 hours a day on social media, between the ages of 39-45 spend 3 hours a day, and between the ages of 50-64, 2.4 hours a day. No wonder it's so hard to get anything done. The time that we could be using to invest in our future to get where we want to be in life we squander on following the lives of celebrities and public figures that have already dedicated themselves to the hard work required to achieve the level of success that we aspire to obtain. And we wonder why we find ourselves in the same place year after year. These practices have become so commonplace, that every day we allow precious time to slip through our hands like the sand in an hourglass. If we are not keenly aware of how we spend our time, it's easy to get distracted and blow huge amounts of time and not even realize it. We live in a day and age where if you are not really careful you could forfeit your entire future wasting time on things that don't truly matter. With the world moving at such a fast pace it is almost inevitable that at some point that most people will fall victim to distraction.

THE COST OF DISTRACTION

Technology is just one of the ways that we get distracted, anything that takes your focus away from achieving the goals that you have set for yourself is a distraction. Distractions come in many forms. Some come disguised as good opportunities, urgent obligations, unanticipated obstacles, fruitless relationships and even gossip. The truth of the matter is that any time that you are doing anything of significance, there will always be an opposition trying to prevent you from achieving greatness. And a lot of times that opposition is an internal struggle between what you want to do and what you know you need to be doing. Which is why self-discipline is so important. It's important to examine EVERYTHING going on around you to assess whether what you are spending your time on is a distraction or not. Even "good" things can become distractions if they interfere with you achieving your goals. Do you currently have any "good" things going on in your life that are taking you away from the most important things that you should be doing?

To really understand distraction, we have to put it in its proper context. PLAIN AND SIMPLE distraction is your enemy. It is always present waiting for an opportunity to swoop in and consume you to get you off course to disrupt and sabotage any meaningful work that you may be doing. Its primary assignment is to steal your attention so that you no longer have the discipline and wherewithal to exert the mental energy and focus that's required to meet your goals. Every single day that we wake up, we are faced with the decision to discipline ourselves and focus on what we aspire to accomplish or allow ourselves to slack off and get sucked into the many distractions that are awaiting us. Every single day, distraction has an opportunity to defeat you! This is a one on one battle between you and the enemy of your destiny. This battle never wanes, never lightens up, and is one you will face every day your feet touch the floor when you get out of bed. Either it will overcome you, or you will overcome it. It's as simple as that there is no way around it. As one writer puts it, we spend our time chasing skinny rabbits, and the reward never compares to what we give up in the process, squandering our time on things that hold no real value in the end.

Time is one of, if not the most precious commodities that we have. Once time is spent, you can never get it back. That's why it's important to stay cognizant of the fact that there is a window of opportunity associated with some dreams that we have and when that time has elapsed so has the dream with it.

OVERCOMING DISTRACTION

The first step to overcoming distraction is becoming aware of the many ways that you get distracted. It's important to study yourself to examine your tendencies to pinpoint the times and circumstances in which you are most likely to get distracted. It is hard to defeat and overcome anything that you are not aware of, which is why the studying self is so important. Once you pinpoint what is distracting you, you can devise a plan to do something about it. You may be amazed at what you find when you invest the time to do the research. Some of the things that you realize are distracting you may be difficult to let go of. Let's keep it real; it can be pretty hard at to pull yourself away from distractions especially when they come in the form of things that we really enjoy. That's why it is so important to evaluate how you spend your time to assess whether or not what you are spending your time on is worth it. You may find that not all things that you devote time to need to be permanently cut from your life, some may just need to be re-prioritized in order of most important.

But in order to do any of that, we have to be brutally honest with ourselves about whether the things we engage in are distractions or not. Most people are not willing to be honest with themselves because it can be a difficult thing to admit and accept responsibility for an area of your life that needs to be addressed. But when we fail to address the distractions in our lives, we, in essence, say that they are more important than the things that we really want. We may not look at it like that but what you truly want always shows up in your actions. You can say what you want out your mouth all day, but if your actions do not line up with what it is that you say that you want, you are only lying to yourself. And the worst person to lie to is yourself.

This is why distraction has to be addressed head-on. If you want to be successful at anything, it is important to get to a point where you can discipline yourself to deny the lure of what you want right now for what you really want in the long run.

I know that adopting this new discipline can seem challenging and make you question if this is even possible for you, but I need you to understand that this process is a gradual process and not something that just happens overnight. It is usually something that you have to work on over time to become better at, and the more you do it, the more you become better at it. Most people don't just go from being undisciplined to disciplined with their time, although it is possible. What is important though, is to begin to notice when you are lending your time to things that won't help you get closer to your goals so that you can begin to redirect yourself to what you should be doing. At the end of the day, it's about what really holds value to you. And you will always know what you truly value by what you spend your time doing. So if your goals are what you value, you have to find the discipline to make yourself do the things that you should be doing. Nobody can do this for you; this is an internal discipline that you have to develop within yourself. There are times now when my friends or even my family are doing things that I would like to be doing that are not consistent with my goals, and I have to decline so that I can stay focused on achieving my goals. Goals don't just accomplish themselves; it takes a great deal of discipline to get to your goals. And oftentimes you will have to make sacrifices to get there.

What I had to do was begin to look at what was consuming most of my free time and make a decision to reduce the amount of time that I was squandering on things that didn't matter. What I figured out was that I needed to reduce the amount of time that I watched television and spent on social media. Not because I no longer enjoyed these things, but because, I had to choose between entertaining myself and doing what really meant the most to me. To make these sacrifices are not always easy but they are necessary if you want to be successful. Life is about sacrifice, one of the things that I have learned is that in order to get something better, you always have to give something up in the process. And the sad truth is this, some people will never have what they want in life because of what they are unwilling to give up. As crazy as that sounds, the only thing that is standing in between many people having what they want out of life are the distractions that they are unwilling to get rid of. I know this all too well because the person that I am describing was once me. I watched day after day, month after month, and year after year go by with me staying stuck in place barely moving forward because of things that I valued more than my destiny. At the time I didn't see it that way, but that was the truth because I put these things before doing what I should have been doing to have what I said I wanted. I was under the illusion that I could do both. I thought I could entertain my distractions and still have what I wanted out of life. It wasn't until time kept getting past me as I began to get older and older seeing missed opportunity after missed opportunity. Then reality hit me in the face like a brick wall. I had to face the truth finally. The cold hard truth is, I had to make a decision; it was either one or the other. It was either I could remove my distractions and go after my destiny, or I could continue to entertain them and accept my current situation at that time as my permanent destiny. I had no choice; there was no in-between. And what I'm telling you is that there is no choice, no in-between, you have to choose one or the other. So what is it going to be? Because you can't do both! You have to make a decision right here right now to choose what means more to you! If being successful means more to you, you will have to do the things that success demands of you, if not, continue to allow yourself to be distracted and accept your fate. But if you do choose to allow distractions to be more important than your dreams, do us all a huge favor don't complain about it. Don't complain about not having the life that you wanted because you chose this fate for yourself and nobody wants to hear your complaints. You had options, you could've chosen otherwise, but you decided what you chose, so do the admirable thing and live with the consequences of not disciplining yourself.

But on the other hand, if you are truly ready to get to that next level, I want you to do a simple assignment for me. I want you to self-assess your own life and identify all of the distractions in your life, and write out a list of the things that you know you must give up to get to the next level. The next thing that I want you to do is to slowly but surely start reducing the amount of time that you spend on the things that are not getting you closer to your dreams and replace that time doing the things that you should be doing that will help you get where you want to go in life.

The more that you begin to do that, the more you will become productive. Things that have eluded you for years will begin to be at your fingertips. Goals that were off far in the distance will become near. And it will become easier to accomplish the things that you want to achieve. This is not just some fancy theory that I have read about, I have personally experienced this in my own life. In this past year, I have accomplished more than I have within the entire last decade. This didn't just happen by happenstance, this occurred as a result of deliberately removing distractions from my life that were holding me back. When I did that, it freed me up to do all the things that I needed to do to become successful.

The last thing that I would like to suggest regarding defeating distraction is putting checks and balances in place. What I mean is, creating an actual plan to overcome them. For example, if you know that you get distracted by social media and the internet on your phone, you may want to turn your phone off while you are completing tasks. Your main objective is to reduce any opportunities of you being distracted. You know yourself better than anyone, so whatever plan you create to hold yourself accountable has to be based on the areas that you find that you get distracted most. Although distraction can be very challenging to overcome, it is not impossible. There are human beings just like you and I that face the same distractions that we do daily, but make the conscious decision to discipline themselves to choose what they want most over what they want right now.

PROCRASTINATION

THE ENEMY OF PROCRASTINATION

Another dream killer that is equally detrimental to your future is the dream killer of procrastination. You know that thing that you have meant to get around to, but it just never happens? I know you know what I'm talking about; let's be honest, we've all been there.

We have all experienced times in our lives where we have put off doing what we knew we needed to be doing until a later date and later never happened. A person that's not truly committed to what it is that they say they want will find any reason to procrastinate. To be honest with you, there are several reasons that people procrastinate and drag their feet when it comes to going after their dreams. The reasons and or excuses vary from person to person, but at the end of the day, they are just that excuses. Because anything that you truly want out of life you can get if you are persistent. Don't get me wrong, you may have some obstacles that you have to overcome in order to get to your goal, but like my elders used to tell me, where there is a will there's a way. You may have to start small and build up your goal. But as long as you consistently take steps towards reaching your goals, you will arrive there at some point. Just like a distraction, procrastination has a huge impact on our lives and our ability to achieve our goals which is why we have to make every effort to remove anything that stands in the way of us fulfilling our dreams.

THE COST OF PROCRASTINATION

Procrastination is very dangerous, and we must look at it as an enemy to our dreams and aspirations. While we put off our dreams, they are slipping farther and farther away from us. Sometimes we take for granted that tomorrow is promised to us when in actuality we don't know when the days that we have been allotted on this earth will be over. That in and of itself should be motivation for us to strive to be our very best selves. Wouldn't it make sense for us to use this precious life that we've been blessed with to experience the fullness of life? To be our best selves? To conquer all that we put our mind to? Sadly, many people will never experience this type of life; they will die as unused potential never knowing what their life might have become had they disciplined themselves to go after their dreams. Potential is simply talents and gifts that our creator has given us that we have not developed and tapped into yet. I once heard a motivational speaker say that contrary to popular belief that the richest place on the planet is the graveyard. In the graveyard, you will find many gifts, talents, and dreams that were never actualized. Many of people have gone to the grave with ideas, concepts, and patents that the world will never benefit from. More importantly, that they will never benefit from them. I bet if we could bring those same people back from the dead, they would urge us to use the short time that we have here wisely.

When we procrastinate, we miss out on so many opportunities known and unknown. There are so many opportunities out there waiting to be claimed, but unless we take action, they will forever elude us. Just like I mentioned with distractions, it's important to know yourself enough to know not only why you procrastinate but all the ways you do. So, in an attempt to get you to identify some of the ways that you may struggle with procrastination, I have listed some of the most common reasons why people procrastinate.

Over the course of my studies, I have compiled a list of the top 5 reasons people procrastinate; let's explore them together.

1. **Lack of Motivation** - Many people don't act on their goals and dreams simply because they don't feel motivated to do so. If you wait until you feel motivated to start a task, you will never start. This is particularly true when you find the task challenging or uninteresting. People tend to think that at some point, there is some magical feeling that will overtake you and you will magically feel inspired to do all that you have ever dreamed or imagined. Life simply does not work that way. There is always something more exciting or enjoyable that you could be doing with your time rather than working, but without sowing, there is no reaping. What I have found to be true is quite the opposite, once you begin doing, you will then find the motivation to do more. It's like getting back in the gym after a long hiatus. The first day is always the hardest, if you can just get past that first day, then it will make it easier to come back for a second day, then a third day, and before you know it, you find motivation to continue based on the progress that you are seeing. Progress is the reward of consistency. But in order to get to that point, it all starts with overcoming every excuse that you have rationalized why you could put off starting that first day. Many people want to know the secret to finding motivation. And while many different things motivate different people, it is very important to identify your own personal reason to go after your dreams. What is your "WHY?" What will motivate you to never give up despite whatever comes your way? What is it that you can hold on to that will motivate you to get out of the bed on those days where life has thrown everything but the kitchen sink at you? That's where the real work begins. It's about looking at your life and figuring out why it's so important for you to invest every fiber of your being into accomplishing what you aspire to accomplish. For me, it's about being able to provide for my

children and not have our options limited due to lack of financial resources. It's about securing a foundation to pass down to not only my children but their children so that they can have a leg up in life that I didn't have. I want to be able to make my own schedule to be available and able to do things like go to my field trips without being subjected to someone else's schedule. It's about living my life in such a way where I can do it on my own terms. That's important to me. So again, my question to you again is, what is your "WHY?" Once you identify what your "WHY" is, the next step is to use that as fuel to ignite the passion needed to go after your dreams. Any time your commitment starts to wane, go back to ground zero and remember "WHY" it is important for you to persevere on towards your goals.

2. **Being Overwhelmed** - Have you ever decided that you wanted to go after a dream or goal and got sidetracked by life's responsibilities? I believe we all have at some point. We are all well-meaning and have a sincere desire to meet the goals and deadlines that we have set for ourselves; then life shows up. I mean really shows up. The list of things that we are responsible for seems to grow and grow and grow. From school, to work responsibilities, to chauffeuring the kids to their various extracurricular activities, to home life and personal relationships. It's like we run through life juggling responsibility after responsibility while trying to maintain our sanity, and before we know it, that thing that we meant to get around to gets lost in the shuffle. The things that we have on our plate end up taking precedence over the things that we want most out of life. If we are not careful, we can get so bombarded with daily tasks that we never set time aside to go after the dreams and goals that could transform our entire lives as well as the people that are connected to us.

Let me first start off by acknowledging how challenging it can be to juggle all of life's responsibilities. When I say, I know what it's like, I really do. For the better part of the last decade, I have had to juggle 2 jobs, a family, and whatever else life threw my way all while working to establish myself professionally. So, I can empathize with how heavy the load that you are carrying may feel right now. But despite everything that you have on your plate right now, you can and must find a way to go after your dreams and aspirations. Because the reality is, if you don't find a way to go after your dreams, you will stay stuck in the rat race of life expending high amounts of energy with minimal returns on your efforts. Some people work really hard building another man's dream while letting theirs fall by the wayside. Wouldn't it make sense that if you are going to work hard day in and day out that you work hard for a dream that's yours? A dream that will allow you to live the life you want to live? Or will you allow your inability to definitively commit to a course of action to pursue your dreams be the reasons that you forfeit your future? Each moment that you procrastinate takes you farther and farther away from achieving your goals.

A lot of times when people procrastinate, the mindset is I'll get to it tomorrow, but tomorrow never comes. Subconsciously, we think that we will wait until the right time when the conditions are right. But guess what? There is never a time when the conditions are right. The conditions become right when you look yourself squarely in the face and say, "You know what you have been procrastinating and making excuses as to why you can't go after your dreams and that must change now." And then commit that no matter what, you will begin to progressively work towards your dream. Even if you start by researching what you must do to pursue your dream, you have taken a proactive step to start your process. Often time's research is the first step that we must take to educate ourselves in our desired field so that we can chart a course of action. And what most people won't tell you is that the process is not complicated as we sometimes imagine it to be in our heads. A lot of times starting the process to go after your dreams is as simple as getting a pad and a pen, looking at your goals and writing down all foreseeable steps to get there. Once you have charted out your course of action, the initial work is done. From that point forward, your responsibility is to just to take action on working your plan. Now, will everything always happen the way you have listed on your plan? No, but the beauty of it is, as you begin your journey, you will constantly be learning and as you do you will be able to make adjustments. There are times when you will have to go back and re-order your steps based on what you have learned, but I have come to realize that as long as you stay open to the unlimited possibilities of Divine wisdom that you will never be steered wrong. Things will just begin to fall into place. You don't need to know all the answers to get started, all you need to do is to respond to the call of that unsettling desire that is in your heart that won't allow you to rest until it is manifested in you. If you do that, God will take care of the rest. All of the resources and people needed to facilitate the dream will appear at the right time.

3. **Self-Doubt** - A wise man once said that you could never operate beyond your vision of yourself. There is a direct correlation between how you see yourself and how far you can go in life. So, my question to you is how do you see yourself? I'm not talking about the superficial answer that you give somebody when they ask you that question. No, how do you really see yourself? What are some of the internal conversations that go on inside of your head that no one else is privy to? Are your thoughts filled with self-defeating thoughts about your abilities? Or do you feel as if you are fully capable of achieving anything that you put your mind to? The truth of the matter is most people are not willing, to be honest with themselves about how they really see themselves. It can be a very painful thing to admit to yourself that you operate in self-doubt. This is why a lot of people choose to be in denial. It is much easier to lie to ourselves

and put on the facade of a confident person to the outside world rather than admitting that you struggle with self-worth and have created self-imposed limitations as a result of what you believe to be true about yourself.

Self-doubt is dangerous and will make you believe that you are not worthy of the endless possibilities that are out there for you. Where it gets tricky though is that this fight is not always at the conscious level. Sometimes there can be years of messages of unworthiness stored on the hard drives of our minds buried deep within our soul. Messaging that has been planted there by your parents, past relationships, your environment, as well as the dominant society. There is a quote by Carter G Woodson that states, *"If you can control a man's thinking you do not have to worry about his action. When you determine what a man shall think you do not have to concern yourself with what he will do. If you make a man feel that he is inferior, you do not have to compel him to accept an inferior status, for he will seek it himself. If you make a man think that he is justly an outcast, you do not have to order him to the back door. He will go without being told; and if there is no back door, his very nature will demand one."* That is one of the most powerful quotes that I have ever come across. It speaks directly about operating in self-doubt and how you become incapable of carrying out the actions needed to be successful. A lot of people procrastinate because they either think that they are not capable of completing the task or not worthy. Until you believe that you are first of all worthy of greatness and secondly fully capable of achieving anything that you put your mind to, there is nothing that anybody can tell you to help you move forward. It has to come from a deep internal resolve that you are more than capable of achieving greatness. Where people fall short is that they rely on their own abilities, you have to remain aware at all times that you have access to a power greater than yourself operating inside of you. When you tap into that power that is readily available to you, it will transcend your limitations and empower you to do things that you didn't think that you could do.

4. **Fear Of Failure** - Most people that procrastinate as a result of fear of failure may believe that trying hard and failing is worse than never trying at all. For them, it's easier to feel like since I didn't really try hard I didn't really fail. Procrastination is used as a way to protect them from perceived failure. What they don't realize is that whether you work hard and fail or simply never try, you end up in the same place. The problem for people that think this way is that they equate what they do with who they are. Just because you don't succeed at your first time trying something does not mean you're a failure. You simply tried something that didn't work. Failure is only failure when you stop trying. Most successful people will tell you that the road to success wasn't a straight path. The road was filled with many obstacles and setbacks which many would consider failure. The difference between successful people and those that are not is that they don't perceive things not happening exactly as planned as failure, they look at these situations as opportunities to learn from their mistakes and make adjustments that will help them become successful in future endeavors. Look at Tyler Perry, for example, Tyler Perry is one of the most successful filmmakers in all of Hollywood, but it didn't start out that way. Tyler had a rough childhood growing up in New Orleans, Louisiana. Early in his life he experienced abuse at the hands of his father and began writing as an outlet to express himself, and that writing eventually evolved into his first stage play, "I Know I've Been Changed." Tyler saved up his entire life savings of 12,000 to put on his first production. To his surprise, it flopped! Only 30 people came out that first night. Then he went back to the drawing board and continued to put on plays for 7 years all with minimal success while being homeless living in his car. But the thing that allowed him to prevail was holding on to the

belief that all of his travails were going to pay off and it did! At the brink of giving up, he decided to put on one last play. However, in this particular play, he took a different approach. He invited several local choir members to join the cast of the play in an attempt to get the faith-based community to come and see the play which held a strong message of faith. By his own admission that night in the dressing room, he had decided that this was it, that he was going to give up, that he wasn't going to do another play. He said that he heard the voice of God say, "It's not over until I say it's over." He said he looked out the dressing room and to his amazement, the line was around the corner. He said the next night was the same thing. And the next night as well. From that day forward, he has never looked back. He has gone on to write, direct, produce, and act in several more stage plays and feature films. Imagine what would have happened if he never continued to keep going as he stared what most would perceive to be failure directly in the face? Even worse, what would the outcome be if he never tried? The potential for rewards far outweighs the perceived risks. What do you have to lose? If you try and it doesn't turn out the way that you had expected, analyze what went wrong and what you could have done better and use that information to make better informed decisions on the next round. Like the old adage says, the only thing that beats a failure is a try. You would be surprised how far you can get by simply putting in the effort to achieve your goals.

5. **Avoidance of Pain** - Another common reason people procrastinate is because they do not want to endure the pain and hard work that it takes to become successful. To be successful requires a great deal of discipline, focus, and sacrifice that many people are not willing to endure to become what they want to be. The cost is too much; they will have to give too much of themselves, and some people are just not ready for that. They cringe at the thought of being stretched

and having to dig deep to have greatness manifested in them. It is much easier to retreat to their comfort zone where they can manage everything, and not a lot is required of them. If it is, it is an area that they have mastered and that they can easily facilitate. That's why successful people are celebrated in the way that they are, it's not that they are necessarily more talented than anyone else, it's that they were willing to endure the pain of hard work to get where they are. They understand that pain is part of the process and they embrace rather than run from it. If you avoid pain, you will never be successful because you won't be willing to put in the work to get there. It reminds me of the saying that if it were easy everybody would do it because the truth of the matter is that greatness is not easily achieved. There is a saying that says that 2 percent of people in the world have the guts to go after their dreams and the other 98 percent end up working for the 2 percent that dared to believe. What you need to understand is that pain is not permanent, it is temporary, and at the end of pain there is a reward. Think about a woman giving birth to a child; I'm told that it's one of the most excruciating pain that a human can endure. I'm sure that during the process, it feels like the pain is never ending, enduring hours of labor with the body being pushed to limits it never thought of being pushed to. But once the baby is out and the mother looks into the eyes of that beautiful child, at that very moment, all the pain that was endured becomes worth it. And before you know it, the pain is forgotten about as the parents get to relish in the experience of loving on that child. So it is with our dreams; we must endure the pain, toil, and labor of hard work to be able to relish in the rewards of our successes; there is no way around it. Look at it like this, there will be pain whether you quit or if you persevere, so if you are going to go through pain, either way, you might as well get a reward from it.

NAYSAYERS

Earlier in the chapter, we talked about internal dream killers and identifying the things inside of us that threaten our dreams. In this portion of the chapter, I want to talk about some external factors that act as enemies to us fulfilling our destiny. I want to take a second to address one of the biggest deterrents that discourage a lot of people from going after their dreams in life, which are naysayers. In life, there will always be naysayers, haters, and individuals that don't want to see you win. Most of them don't even know why they hate, but life has them so jaded and skeptical of the limitless possibilities that are out there that they hate on anybody that dares to believe in something more than what they can see. You see, one thing about being a visionary is that you will see things that others cannot see, and because they don't have the vision, they will try to limit yours. But what you have to realize is that the vision God gave to you is for you. It doesn't matter if anybody else sees it, you are charged with the task of holding on to it and taking steps to bring it to fruition.

You will be surprised to find out that some of the biggest dream killers and naysayers are those closest to us. Often times naysayers come in the form of family members and close friends and people that you hold near and dear to your heart. What's heartbreaking about that is these are the people that you would expect to support you even more than anyone else but, unfortunately, it doesn't always work that way. The problem with those that know us is that they know us. Those that feel that they know us or even have a long history with us have a hard time seeing us as more than the person that they originally knew. Despite how much we've grown or transformed our lives, people that have not grown themselves tend to want to keep you in a box where you once were. It's comfortable to them; it's the level that they can communicate with you on. Thoughts of you becoming successful magnifies their failure if they are not equally growing. The more you grow, the less you have in common with those that you were once on the same level with. There is a saying that says that two people that can't grow together will eventually grow apart. That is why it is so important to evaluate your circle of influence. If you are surrounded by people that operate on level 2, but you operate on level 10, what can they honestly offer you to support you in going where you're going? As blunt as that may sound, if we are truly honest with ourselves, is it not true? It's not that you are any better than anyone it's just that when you elevate everything, things around you also need to elevate. Sometimes elevation requires separation. There comes a time in life where you may have to make some hard decisions, and that may include separation from family and friends and those that we love. As hard as it may be, it may be necessary for growth. It doesn't mean that you don't love them or are no longer there for them. It just means that you put boundaries on those that you let influence you or speak into your life.

You have to be very careful who you let speak into your life. My favorite book says that power of life and death is in the tongue. Which means that those that you give access to speak to your life can speak either life or death to your destiny. It is that serious, which is why it is even more important who you let advise you. Many people have allowed themselves to be talked out of their dreams by people that couldn't see what they see. The people around them couldn't see it, and they allowed them to make them believe that what they aspired to do was impossible. It's not necessarily that they meant any ill will towards you, a lot of times those that try to talk you out of going after your dreams think that they are helping you. They believe in their heart that they are saving you from perceived failure. Even though their intentions are good, anybody that speaks anything other than life into your dreams is detrimental to your success. This is why you have to really analyze who you lend your ear to as it relates to your future. Make it a point to surround yourself with those that speak life into you and encourage you. Those that stretch you and hold you accountable for doing your best. Those that support you and encourage you should equally be able, to be honest with you about areas where you could require improvement as well. It's important to be open to feedback if we are to get better. There is nothing worse than a person that thinks they know it all. Because a "know it all" leaves no room for growth, and the truth of the matter is to have someone around you that will only tell you what you want to hear is equally as detrimental to your growth as a naysayer. The difference between constructive criticism and negative influence is that constructive criticism if received correctly can empower you to correct areas where you have weaknesses or flaws. However, on the flipside, a negative, fault finding cynical person can shoot down your dreams faster than a fighter jet under enemy attack. So, with that being said, make sure that you choose individuals and environments that are conducive to you achieving your goals. People will always have an opinion of you and what you should be doing, but the only thing that matters is what you think and believe to be true about you.

At the end of the day, it is important to identify and eliminate anything that acts as a barrier in between you accomplishing your goals. I would be lying if I said it was going to be easy, but those that are successful do it every day. That is, even more, motivation to suggest that you can do the same thing. However, in order to make that happen, it's going to require something of you. You will have to give up the comfort of now to have what you want in the future. Success has a price associated with it that must be paid in full. There are no shortcuts or easy routes to get there. You have to decide that what you say you want is of the utmost importance and do the things that are required to have it.

As you pursue your dreams, there will always be people that don't understand your vision who don't want to see you win, and may even try to discourage you from dreaming because they can't do what you do. Do not let this deter you. You must keep on moving forward towards your goals even if it means you are walking alone.

On this journey, you are going to experience haters, you are going to encounter naysayers, but whatever you do you must remain focused on the objectives at hand. Never let their opinions of you matter more than what you think of yourself. Never let what they say about you distract you enough to slow you down, and never let the limitations that they set for you become your own. They may not get your vision right now, but trust me, everybody will get it eventually as your accomplishments will speak for themselves. In closing, I will leave you with this. The only way a dream killer can come in and hinder you from getting to your dreams is if you invite it in and let it take up residence in your life.

PART THREE
ACTION

CHAPTER 7
IT ALL STARTS IN THE MIND

"If you want to change the fruits, you will first have to change the roots. If you want to change the visible, you must first change the invisible."

—T. Harv Eker

Everything, absolutely everything starts in your mind. All that you will ever achieve in life or the lack thereof is in direct correlation to how you think. How you think is the single most deciding factor to the outcome of your life. There is not a single thing that has more of an impact on a person than the way that they see themselves and the world around them. You can usually look at a person's life and guesstimate how they think by the fruits that they produce in their lives. As I have said many times in this book, the only thing that differentiates the successful from the unsuccessful is how they think. Most successful people's minds are focused on what they can do and what they can achieve while most unsuccessful people's thoughts tend to focus on what they can't do and why they can't do them.

The mind is the origin of all things. What you think, what you imagine, what you feel, and what you believe you will create in your life by the repetition of your thoughts. Your mind is where all great things are birthed and where all of your ideas and dreams are cultivated. It is also where lack, poverty, and failure are birthed as well because what you experience in life is just a reflection of what you have been thinking on the inside.

Your mind is the most valuable resource that you have, as it is the vehicle that will transport you to wherever you go in life. Through the power of intentionally developing your mind, you can literally create the destiny that you want for yourself. What many people fail to realize is that, where you currently are in your life, is a direct reflection of the quality of your mind. The healthier your mind is, the more likely you are to achieve great things. The more negative your mind is, the more likely you are to produce negative things. Your mind can either propel you forward or hold you back from getting where you want to go, which is why you have to program your mind for success. While we are faced with many challenges every day, the biggest challenge that you will ever encounter will be to direct your thinking in such a way that it will be consistent with where you want to go. Those that are successful in life were successful in their minds long before their success became tangible. You have to have the ability to see yourself as being successful in your mind's eye long before it becomes tangible. Success is first birthed inwardly and then manifests itself outwardly. So many people attempt to go after big goals and dreams before they have even done the internal work to prepare themselves to be successful.

This really dawned on me as I was running a young men's group a couple of years ago. My co-facilitator and I started a series called Dream Chasers with the goal in mind of inspiring young men to go after their dreams. What we quickly realized as we did all of this work around preparing them to go after their dreams was that we had missed a step in the process. Through our interactions with these young men, we learned that before a person can even begin to do the work of going after their actual dreams, they have to first start by addressing the internal barriers that have held them back. You have to begin by identifying and addressing the self-limiting beliefs that are the real barriers that stand in between you and your goals. For many people, they have to build up the belief and courage that they can actually do what they aspire to do. They have to get to a point where they really believe that what they want is possible for them. That is where the real work starts, which is why mindset development is important. Everybody is not just naturally confident. Everybody does not just know how to go out there and get it. Everybody is not just naturally driven, but these things can be developed, through the intentional and deliberate work of developing your mind.

In this chapter, I would like to introduce to you the concept of mindset development. I would like to discuss the crucial role that it plays in your life and talk about the benefits of developing your mind and the consequences of failing to do so. In this chapter, I will provide you with some practical tips that will support you in the development of your mind as well as show you the dangers of not engaging in such a process.

Mindset development is the intentional and deliberate act of conditioning your mind for success. As I mentioned earlier, you have to be very intentional about programming your mind to do what you want it to do for you. The unprogrammed mind doesn't naturally just go where you want it to go; you have to take control of your mind and make it submit to the direction you want it to go in. The mind is like a sponge; it will absorb whatever is planted in it. If the mind is constantly subjected to doubt and self-defeating thoughts, those things will begin to be manifested in your life. Equally, if your mind is conditioned to believe that nothing is impossible and that you can have whatever you want out of life, then you will begin to create that reality for yourself. Not as a result of just thinking positive alone, but once you believe that something is possible for you, it will then motivate you to take steps to pursue what you feel is obtainable for you. My favorite book in the world states that as a man thinketh so is he, so whatever you think about you become. And becoming what you aspire to be mentally is the first step in it manifesting itself physically.

THE UNDEVELOPED MIND

LIMIT OURSELVES

When we fail to condition our minds, we limit ourselves. We limit ourselves and our ability to grow because anything that you do not feed will wither away and die. We seem to understand this concept when it comes to other things, but we act as if we don't understand this when it comes to developing our minds. How is the mind expected to produce great things when you don't take the time to develop it to do so? When you don't do anything to better yourself or to advance what you already are, the result is stagnation. So many people want to be further along in their lives but are not willing to do anything to make that happen. I guess by luck of chance they figure that they are supposed to just grow without putting in any work to make that a reality. They suffer from the illusion that they will miraculously get where they want to go in life without making the investment to condition the mind to take them there. The mind is the driving force that will take you to your goals. In the same way that not putting gas in a car and expecting it to take you to your destination would be foolish, so is not working on your mind and expecting to have a successful life is. They say that insanity is doing the same things over and over and looking for a different result. If the results that you are producing in your life are less than what you would want them to be, that may be an indication that it is time to do something different. Staying the same, not doing anything different and expecting to see your life become better is fantasy that will not bring about the results that you desire in life. When you don't develop yourself, you limit your growth, your opportunities and your ability to be successful because there is no way to get a return where you have not invested.

YOU NEVER GROW

As crazy as it sounds several people go through life aimlessly never engaging in a process to strengthen and develop themselves mentally. Many people just go through life accepting things the way they are never attempting to have or become more. Just the thought of that makes me cringe, as I can remember a time in my life where I was the same way. I can remember how I felt day in and day out, feeling like how my life was the best that it probably was going to be. Feeling like I was a victim of my circumstance and that my options were limited. A lot of that was based on how I saw myself and the world around me. I saw myself as a young black man, ex-offender and high school dropout with limited options based on some poor decisions that I had made early in my life. It wasn't until I started to work on myself that I began to have the confidence that I could be more. Prior to that, my unwillingness to invest in my own development stunted my growth. I stunted my growth by not taking the necessary steps to become better. Had I started to do the work that I eventually went on to do, I may have started to transform my life much sooner, but I'm a firm believer that everything happens for a reason. But what about the people that never decide to engage in the process of self-development, what do you think the outcome of their lives will be? Imagine all of your life you operated far beneath your ability and went to the grave never knowing what you could have done? Wouldn't that be a tragedy? Wouldn't that be a life wasted? I had an experience like that with my son this football season. At the beginning of the season he was pumped, he had all these plans for how he was going to dominate the season. He talked about how he was going to exploit his matchups and score several touchdowns and then when he got on the field reality hit him like a ton of bricks. Now all of the things that he said he was going to do before the game he had to execute, it was game time. And guess what he did? He played far beneath his ability, and I couldn't understand for the life of me why. Why would somebody with so much enthusiasm about what they are going to do come out and do the opposite? Sound like anybody you know? But at any rate, I just chalked that up to being the first game, but week after week I saw his play decline. He was a wide receiver which means that he is the player that the quarterback throws the ball to. They are responsible for getting open so that they make catches to move the ball. Week after week I would sit back and watch this man run some of the most lackluster routes I have ever seen anybody run in all of my days of watching football. I mean this dude would put in minimal effort expecting to do big things in the game, and he wondered why the quarterback was never targeting him. He was just downright lazy and just didn't put any effort to do what he was capable of doing. I grew increasingly disappointed as I went to game after game and saw him do the same thing. It was just mind-blowing to me because I knew what he was capable of. It wasn't until the last game of the season that I saw something different from him. I went to talk to him before the game; I said this is your last game, what are you going to do? He said I feel different today, I feel like a beast. I said ok, well let's see that translated on the field. So from the first play, he came out with an intensity that I didn't see him have all season. He was running all of his routes hard and guess what, he started getting targeted more. So much so that on one of the drives, he beat his man, went to the end zone but ended up dropping a touchdown. He was devastated because he felt that he might not have another chance to score a touchdown before the last game of his final season. I saw him go to the sideline starting to look defeated, I went over there and told him, "Keep your head in the game if you keep up your intensity it will come." So, he went back out there with his intensity still up playing his heart out in his last game. Deep into the fourth quarter when it looked all but bleak for him to score a touchdown in his last game with 36 seconds left he caught a pass. Determined to score in his final game, he shook one defender off and outran 3 more all snipping at his ankles as he sprinted into the end zone in a way that I have never seen him run before to score a touchdown in his last high school game. All I could think to myself is that he had the ability hidden within him to do that all season. It's just in that last game; he found a reason compelling enough for him to pull out his best. But despite him not playing to that level the whole season, I am glad that he got an opportunity to see what he truly possessed if he put his all in. How many of us will wait until the final seasons of our lives to bring out our best? Or will you wait until there are no more ticks on the clock left and regret what you could have done with your life if you were intentional about the work of developing yourself? The only way that you will become more is by what you invest in you, your mind has the ability to transform your life, that's why you must become obsessed with the work of developing it.

This chapter is not about me and my personal experiences as much as it is about me using my experiences as an example of what happens when you don't intentionally condition your mind. How can you grow? All you know is what you know, so if you don't add anything to that, how can you develop more of a skill set? How can you become more than you currently are? If your mind is the vehicle that will take you wherever you want to go in life, how can that vehicle get you where you want to go if it has no directions and is not properly cared for? In life, there is no such thing as staying the same, either you are becoming better, or you are growing worse. Either you are getting closer to your goal or getting farther away. Every day that you don't work on your mind is a day wasted to move towards your destiny. There is a lot at stake when it comes to mindset development. Your very future depends on it, the quality of your life will never exceed the quality of your mind, so the work of developing your mind is serious business.

SO WHAT ARE YOU GOING TO DO?

With that being said, my question to you today is what are you going to do to develop the quality of your mind? Are you willing to engage in a process to condition your mind for greatness? Or are you just going to hope and wish that by some chance that you can get where you want to go with the information that you have now? Has the information that you currently have allowed you to experience the level of success that you want to achieve? Could there be some information that if you had it, could transform your entire life? Like I mentioned in previous chapters, the only difference between the wealthy and those that are not is the information that they have. The wealthy understand that it's important to be a lifelong learner. You can never have enough information; things are constantly changing and evolving. Especially living in the information age, things are always changing, upgrading and modifying. There is always a better, more efficient way to do things. Think back to the first iPhone, which was like one of the most revolutionary things that we had ever seen. But now eight models later if you looked at what the current iPhone can do versus the first one, it's like night and day. Things are always changing, so to keep up we must equally evolve with the change that's going on around us. That's just to keep up not to mention being cutting edge. So again, my question to you is, are you really ready to put in the work to get where you want to go? Many people say they do, but not many are willing to go through the process to get there. And constantly developing your mind is part of the process to get there. To be cutting edge, to be a leader in your field or industry, you must know things that other people don't know and present it in a way that it's never been presented. There are too many carbon copies out there. To make a big splash, you must obsess yourself with gathering information for the purpose of executing your goals. The beautiful thing about developing your mind is that you begin to feel empowered by doing so. You begin to see things differently, you start to see the world differently, and more importantly, you begin to see yourself differently. There is really no way to explain what happens to a person that is constantly absorbing positive, uplifting and encouraging information. The information will provide direction, clarity, and instruction on how to reach your goals if you are willing to do the hard work to get there.

MINDSET DEVELOPMENT

I guess the million dollar question is, how do you begin to develop your mind? Many people never engage in the process of developing their minds because they simply don't know where to start. In this portion of the chapter, I want to share with you five different strategies that I have personally used that if applied to your life will empower you to condition your mind for success.

RETRAIN YOUR MIND

To recondition your mind, you must first start off by looking at the condition of your mind. It's important to examine the state of your mind to evaluate if your thinking is conducive to where you are trying to go in life. Although it may be hard, it is crucial to have the ability to self-assess areas of your life that need improvement. Many people struggle with self-assessment because it is often hard to be brutally honest with yourself and accept things about yourself that you may not like. In addition to that, many people are oblivious to areas of their lives that require change. It's hard to see the full picture when you are in the frame. Sometimes we need objective people that have our best interest at heart to give us feedback about areas that we need to address. That person could be someone who we really trust their opinion or maybe even a professional. My main point in all of this is that the starting point of retraining your mind is seeing the need to do so. You must see the benefit of upgrading your thinking, that's not to say that there is anything wrong with your thinking now, but every now and then getting updated software downloaded to the hard drives of our minds wouldn't hurt either.

Mindset development is as much about taking negative things out of your mind as it is about putting the positive in. In order to have a healthy mind, you have to begin to retrain your mind by identifying your limiting beliefs and replacing those beliefs with affirming, empowering beliefs about yourself. Initially, it may feel uncomfortable but do it again and again and again until you actually start to believe the things that are true about yourself. This is hard work, and it won't come naturally. You have to be intentional and deliberate about feeding yourself the truth religiously so much so that the information that you absorb becomes your new truth, and that brings me to my next point which is the importance of feeding your mind.

FEED YOUR MIND

In order to expand your vision and condition your mind for success, you have to be very intentional about what you feed your mind. Like I mentioned earlier in the chapter, mindset development is the intentional, deliberate act of feeding your mind with content that will empower you to become better. What content should one ingest? I'm glad that you asked. There are a number of things that you can ingest to begin to build up your mind, ranging from spiritual literature to self-help and the likes. What's most important is that you consume something that will build you up and edify you daily. And it's not just limited to reading. You can read books, listen to audiobooks, listen to podcasts, watch videos, etc. The important things are that you get in a regular habit of feeding your mind. When you ingest empowering content, it just does something to your spirit. Imagine a child growing up in a home where from the time they are born they are told that they are destined for greatness. They are told that they can do all things and that whatever they want to accomplish is within reach. Then they have an example of somebody that is successful modeling that success is attainable for them. What do you think will happen to that child? Do you think that then consuming positive information daily will aid them in their pursuit of success? Do you think the positive affirmations about who they are and what they can accomplish will empower their thinking about their abilities? The same rings true for you and I. We may not have an actual person that will pour into us in that way, but we have access to any kind of information that we want at our fingertips. You can go to the internet right now and receive anything that you need, from motivational content to how-to instructions that take you from A to Z on how to complete whatever task you may be engaged in. The real question is, what are you going to do with the resources out there? There are a number of tools out there to aid and abet you in building yourself up for FREE. You don't have to pay a dime to get this content; you can go to YouTube and access life-changing information from some of the greatest minds that have ever walked the earth RIGHT NOW! But the thing is, it's not going to come to you, you have to go out there and get it. My suggestion is that you start out by taking the time to consume something edifying every single day for 30 days as a project to see if it has any impact on the quality of your mind. Again, the content can be in any form that you prefer; book, motivational videos, podcast, sermons, audio books, whatever, the important thing is that you intentionally feed your mind information every single day that will build upon the quality of your mind. If you do this for 30 days without ceasing, I guarantee you that the impact that it will have on your life will be mind-blowing.

ALIGN YOURSELF WITH THE RIGHT PEOPLE

Who you align yourself with is critical in your pursuit of becoming successful. Linking yourself to the right people can make all the difference in the world. I owe a great deal of the knowledge that I have to the people that have poured into my life. From mentors to coaches and Pastors that I have had the privilege to sit under and learn from. I can't tell you where my life would've been without these people. And I'm even more thankful for the teachers to come. No man is an island, and no one knows everything themselves. We could all learn and benefit from others that are doing the things that we aspire to do. Mentors can come into your life and provide you with information that can transform your life. Mentorship and tutelage are important. It's essential to learn from their successes as well as their failures. Most people only focus on learning from others' successes. But there is some benefit from learning from their failures as well. Learning from the failures of somebody that has gone before us provides us with information on what not to do. When you learn what not to do, you can avoid the unnecessary pitfalls that may await you. Learning from this viewpoint enables you to see things from a much broader perspective.

And when you see things from a broader perspective, you can make more informed decisions. The beauty in aligning ourselves with like-minded people is that it can be very motivating and inspiring. It can provide a network of support as well as accountability that you may not have on your own. Aligning yourself with the right people will do one of two things, either it will motivate you to go hard and take no prisoners when it comes to getting everything that you came for, or it will cause you to get out of the way and make room for those that really want it. There is no in between. On the road to success, there is no hand-holding. Your grind will bring you into the presence of those trying to get it like you, or your idleness will alienate you from individuals that have the ability to come into your life and inspire you for the better.

INVEST IN YOURSELF

In life, people invest in a lot of things. People invest in everything from cars, clothes, homes, and whatever else they find appealing. But very rarely do people take the time to invest in their minds. The difference between successful people and those that are not is those that are successful understand the importance of investing in their minds. What is the last thing you have done to invest in your mind? If it came down to you spending money to increase your skill set or buying that outfit that you want, how would you choose to spend your money? Most people would give into the emotion of the instant gratification of buying the outfit rather than investing in their minds. My question is and always will be, which will benefit you more in the long run? On any given day, the investment in your mind will by far benefit you more than spending your money on something that will depreciate as soon as you use it. We should take every opportunity to invest in the betterment of ourselves. My question to you right now this very moment is, what can you do to invest in yourself? Are there any courses or workshops in your area that offer an opportunity for you to sharpen your gift or learn more about what you aspire to do? Are there any online communities that you can join that will hold you accountable for what you say you want to do? Are there any seminars or conferences that are coming to your area that you can attend that would provide you with information to sharpen your thought process and prepare you for your goals? These are just some of the questions to consider when thinking about investing in yourself. Some of the investments that you make may not require money but an investment of your time or other resources that you may have. Are you ready to part with your time, sometimes depriving yourself of your sleep? Are you ready to forgo some of the activities that you enjoy to invest in yourself? If you are not, you are not ready to be great. The whole act of investing in your dream requires you to give up everything to eventually get everything that you really want in the long run. You have to invest every fiber of your being in pursuing your goals. People often talk about what you have to give up, but the investment is equally as large. What are you willing to do to get where you want to go in life? Are you willing to invest time, energy, and money into this opportunity that you have to get what you want out of life? Or, do you think you can get by with minimal investment and get a maximum reward? If you think that this is how it works, you are in for a rude awakening. At the end of the day, if you are going to invest in anything, your wisest investment would be to invest in yourself because you and only you have control of the outcome of that investment.

PROTECT YOUR MIND

As important as it is for you to feed your mind, it is equally as important to guard and protect your mind from things that don't support your growth. As you work to become the best version of yourself, it is important to eliminate anything from your mind that doesn't empower you to go in the direction that you want to go in. It's already a full-time job to consistently consume things that build you up to go after your goals, to ingest anything contrary to that is counterproductive. What we have to do is begin to eliminate anything and everything that is not in alignment with where we want to go. You have to make the determination that where I want to go in my life is far more important than the recreation or entertainment that would hinder my progress. Now

I'm not suggesting that you shouldn't indulge in entertainment or recreation because there is a time and place for everything, but the bulk of your time should be spent chasing your dream. Like the entertainment mogul Sean "P Diddy Combs" says if you are still chasing your dream, you are not running fast enough. What many people don't understand is that there is a preparation process that one must engage in before their gift is put on display. If you haven't adequately prepared your gift, then when the opportunity to walk in your gift arises, it won't be developed enough to execute the way that you should. One of the ways to squander your opportunity is by ingesting garbage. I have to discipline myself every day because I could easily get caught up and spend large amounts of time watching television and on the net consuming things that don't benefit me. These things are indeed entertaining, but after the entertainment is done, what have I benefited? You have to be on guard what you allow to enter into your mind because although we look at many things as being innocent, these same things can have a great deal of influence on us. What you ingest is a big deal and don't let anybody tell you it's not! Have you ever watched a food commercial and then suddenly became hungry? Or saw a model or one of your favorite celebrities wearing an item that you decided that you just had to have? That's the power of persuasion. Items are marketed to us with the intention of getting us in those stores to buy them because companies understand the power of persuasion. If you see something enough times that interests you, chances are at some point, you will want to get it. It's not only what we see either, you also have to be conscientious of protecting your ear gate as well. Have you ever heard a song and it provoked an emotion in you? You know that workout song that gets you amped before a workout? Or that song that makes you sad or brings up certain memories every time you hear it? The point that I'm simply trying to make is that what you ingest has a great impact on you. With that being said, it is important to protect yourself from ingesting anything that does not build you up to execute your goals. Your mind is your most valuable asset, it would only be wise to protect it.

Mindset development is more about ingesting information that will encourage you, strengthen you, and build you up more than it is just to learn a skillset or a particular way to do something. Man, I can't tell you where my life would've been without listening to sermons, podcasts, reading books, and just putting myself in a space to be motivated and inspired by great thinkers. That literally changed my entire life. I even have funks where my thinking is not the best now. But what I always do is go back to ground zero and fill myself with things that reignite my flame, that make me feel like I can press on. You would be amazed at what the right information could do to your life. The good book states that faith comes by hearing. What are you hearing? What are you seeing? What are you ingesting? Never underestimate the power that what you ingest has on you. Think about what happens when you hear that one song that just gets you pumped every time that you hear it? You could be anywhere, but when that song comes on, you jump out of your seat and are instantly feeling it. What about that movie that you see that every time you see it, it invokes a certain kind of emotion in you? What you ingest is powerful. That's why they say to guard your ear gate and your eye gate always because what you ingest could change your whole life. In the same way, those things have an impact on us so will the right things when we ingest them. Investing in the development of your mind is crucial to your success because without doing so, you will forever be limited in what you can do because you are only as good as what you know.

If there is anything that I can impress upon you, it's the importance of continually working on the development of your mind. Your mind is the vehicle that will take you to the places that you desire to go in life, so always make it a priority to invest in it because as your mind grows so will every other area of your life. You don't have to come in knowing everything that it takes to get to your destination, all you have to do is commit yourself to the process of lifelong learning, and the things that you need to know will be made known to you. Mindset development is a lifelong process and the more you invest, the more you will see a benefit in your life. Always make every effort to be your best and never neglect to invest in your growth.

CHAPTER 8
SACRIFICE FOR SUCCESS

"The man that is not willing to sacrifice
will never have more than he is willing to give up"

—Edward L. Moore

If **you were** to interview several successful people on what made them successful, undoubtedly, they would have similar stories of what they did to get where they are. You may hear things like it took hard work, dedication, and consistency. You may hear them say that they had to be relentless in the face of opposition and never give up. They may tell you a whole host of things that they had to do, but I guarantee you that every one of them will tell you that they had to sacrifice something to get where they are. You see, those that accomplish great things understand the importance of sacrifice. They understand that in order to have more, sometimes you have to give something up. And they are ok with that because their focus is more on what they want in the future than what it is that they have to give up in the present. Having the discipline to sacrifice what you want now for what you want in the future is what separates the successful from the unsuccessful. If you want to do anything great in life, it will come at a price and will require some sacrifice to get where you want to go. But that's where the problem lies. Most people don't want to go through the rigors of day in and day out disciplining themselves and giving up things that they want even if they know that there is a reward at the end of the tunnel. The future often seems so far off, and it is so much easier to give in to the temptation of what you want right now. After all, if you give in to what you want right now, that's instantaneous gratification. But to deprive yourself of what you want now for delayed gratification takes real restraint and most people simply are not willing to go through the discomfort of sacrifice to achieve success. Instead of allowing their vision of where they want to ultimately be the driving force behind their decisions, they end up giving in to their desires of the moment. When you give in to your desires, you may feel good at the moment, but after it's all said and done, there is a price to pay. And often times, the consequence is not becoming the person that you want to become and having the things that you want to have out of life. And I'm not just talking about monetarily, but what you aspire to achieve most. That is a hefty price to pay for not having the discipline to wait for delayed gratification.

In this chapter, we will explore the necessity of disciplining yourself to sacrifice what you want now for what you ultimately want in the long run. We will also examine the consequences of not sacrificing, as well as provide you with insight on how sacrifice is tied directly to your success. When you decide that you want to be successful, you must consider the cost of what it is that you say you want to do. If you are willing to pay the price to get it, you can have it, but if you say you want something but are not willing to do what is required to have it, then you are just spewing rhetoric. Do you really want what you say you want? Or are you merely wishing for what you want in theory with no real intention to put in the action to bring it to fruition? There is a price to pay for what you say that you want. Have you considered the cost?

SUCCESS REQUIRES SOMETHING OF YOU/ NO SHORTCUTS

There is a famous quote by JJ Watt, NFL superstar defensive lineman of the Houston Texans that says, "Success isn't owned it's leased. And every day the rent is due." This quote is so profound in that it speaks directly to the reality that in order to be successful, there is something that is required of you. You must be willing to give up something to get something even greater in return. No matter how you try to manipulate this law, there is simply no way around it. It's just like the law of sowing and reaping; you can't reap where you have not sown. Similarly, you cannot get in life without giving. And that is a principle that you can apply to almost anything. In life, you will only receive the degree that you are willing to give. Many people try to manipulate this law only to end up discouraged and frustrated that their life is not what they want it to be. And no matter how mad you get or how much you try to get something, without giving anything you will end up in the same place time after time. You cannot circumvent the process. There is a process of order to achieving things, and nobody is above it. The more that you try to resist it, it will push back against you. You can try any method that you want to try to manipulate this process, but there is a price to be paid for success. There are no shortcuts and rent is due every day. This is one of the major stumbling blocks between people having success or staying stuck in place. You have to be willing to sacrifice the person that you are to become the person that you want to be to get you where you want to go.

THE SACRIFICE OF SELF

Are you willing to sacrifice who you are to become who you need to be to obtain your goals? Wait! Before you answer that I want you to consider the cost. In order to do this, I want you to consider if you are willing to pay the cost of sacrificing yourself. In order to sacrifice the old you that didn't serve you, you will need to be willing to sacrifice the following aspects of yourself.

1. **How You Think**- Your current mindset has only taken you as far as you currently are. To get to the next level, you will have to begin to stretch the boundaries of your mind and challenge your old way of thinking to become more. If you are not where you want to be and feel like there is more for you, I challenge you to expand your thinking. Your best thinking may have gotten you to the level that you are currently at; however, to get to higher levels, it may require a shift in the way that you think.

2. **What You Believe**- As I mentioned with sacrificing how you think, you must also challenge what you believe. It's so very important to examine what you believe because your beliefs govern your actions. If I believe that people with my background don't achieve high levels of success, then subconsciously I will never do the things that are required to be successful because internally I believe that this is not possible for me. So you have to examine the beliefs that you subscribe to and be willing to sacrifice the ones that don't serve you.

3. **Your Habits**- Merriam dictionary defines habits as a behavior pattern acquired by frequent repetition or physiologic exposure that shows itself in regularity or increased facility of performance. It also goes on to say that habits are: An acquired mode of behavior that has become nearly or completely involuntary. To summarize it plainly, habits are the things that we do regularly and repetitively. Habits can become so much a part of our lives that we do them without thinking. To go a step further, if we are not careful, the habits that we develop in life can gain so much control over us that we begin to do them involuntarily. When is the last time you took the time to examine your habits? You may be surprised at what you see when you take the time to sit down and look at what the sum total of your habits are. Gandhi once said that our beliefs become our thoughts, our thoughts become our words, our words become our actions, our actions become our habits, and our habits become

our character, and our character becomes our destiny. Your habits have such a profound impact on your life that they ultimately shape your entire destiny.

TO LOSE IS TO GAIN

The man that is not willing to sacrifice will never have more than what he is willing to give up. Having an unwillingness to sacrifice where you are now for where you want to be in the long run will eventually leave you with a life full of regrets. There will simply be many accomplishments that you will forfeit because you are not willing to let go of what you need to let go of to get where you want.

The truth of the matter is that you have to really examine where your values lie because that is where you will place your importance and invest your time. If you place too much value on the wrong things, you will always put them before what you need to do to get where you want to go. Every single day, I have to sacrifice things that I would rather be doing to continue to focus on and carry out my goals and dreams. I used to be a fixture in front of the television every night watching hour after hour of tv. And to be honest, I enjoyed it. I still enjoy television in those rare instances when I get an opportunity to watch it. I can't tell you the last time that I really watched tv because the goal of where I want to be has become more important than the pleasure I get indulging in watching television. Until you find something that is more important than the things that you currently place value on, you will continue to put those things over the things that you need to do to get where you want to go in life. I'd much rather invest my time and energy to be the one that has reached a level of prestige and prominence for being an expert in my field than someone who watches someone else living out their dreams.

Every day that we do that, we lose valuable time that we can never get back. It's just like I talked about in earlier chapters; you have to really be disciplined because there are so many distractions out there. Listen, I know the distractions are pleasurable, I know that they help you pass the time. I know that everyone else is doing it, but that is exactly why there is 98% of the population working for the 2% that chose to deny themselves on the front end to have what they wanted for the rest of their lives.

What is it that you need to give up to reach your goals and dreams uninterrupted? It will be something different for each person based on your life and conditions. I suggest you do a self-inventory and honestly evaluate your life and be honest with yourself about what's standing in the way of your destiny. It may be distractions like social media, television, and talking on the telephone or it may be unhealthy relationships and people that you need to sacrifice. Everybody can't go where you are going, and until you release them, they will be the anchor that holds you down. There is a saying that says that elevation requires separation and there is nothing wrong with that. The longer you live and the more you realize the effect of having the wrong people around you, you will become more willing to forsake those relationships to move into your destiny unhindered.

Sacrifice is tough, and nobody wants to give up things that they either hold near and dear to their heart or enjoy, but you have to consider, is this thing more important than me getting to where I want to go in life? If the answer is no, no matter how hard it is, you have to be willing to let it go! So, I ask you again, what is it that you need to give up to get where you want to go?

WHAT HAS TO GO IN ORDER FOR ME TO GROW?

Hopefully, this chapter has gotten you to begin thinking about what it is that you need to sacrifice to become successful. Hopefully, it has created a sense of urgency for you to remove anything from your life that acts as an obstacle between you and your goals. A good starting place to assess the sacrifices you need to make is by asking yourself a series of questions to determine the things in your life that you may need to sacrifice. I have put together a list of questions that if answered honestly, could serve as a starting point for you to identify and take accountability for the things in your life that must go. Some people are simply unaware of the areas they need to sacrifice, so I have created an exercise for the purpose of identifying the areas of sacrifice.

THE INSTRUCTIONS ARE AS FOLLOWS:

It is critical that you get a pen and paper and go through each question individually to identify as many answers that you can of areas that you need to sacrifice in order to get where you want to go. It is important to go through each question as thoroughly as possible to elicit as many answers to the questions as you can. Remember, these questions will act as the starting point of you getting rid of the things that are standing between you and your destiny. The more effort that you put into this, the more you will get out of it.

BELOW IS A SACRIFICE ASSESSMENT LIST: QUESTIONS

1. Am I willing to make the difficult choices necessary to be successful?
2. What habits or things must I sacrifice to get to my goals?
3. What habits or things could actually stop me from getting to my goals?
4. What will happen if I don't make the necessary sacrifices to get where I want to go?
5. How could I be better using my time?
6. What things could I be investing my time and resources into that would help me get closer to my goals?
7. Who are some of the people that I have to let go of to get where I want to go?
8. What about myself, am I going to have to change to get to my goals?
9. What resources do I need to make these changes?
10. How will I actually go about making these changes?

REMOVING THE ROADBLOCKS THAT IMPEDE SUCCESS
WEIGH OUT WHAT'S IMPORTANT

Now that you have had a chance to identify some of the things that you need to sacrifice to get to your goals, how was that process for you? I bet you saw some things that may feel really hard for you to let go of, as well as some things that are a little easier for you to give up. The truth of the matter is that people become more willing to sacrifice when what they want becomes more important than what they will have to give up to get what they want. You know we say we want a lot of things and may feel as if we earnestly mean it, but there is a saying that says, what you want shows up in your actions not in what you say.

The first place to start when choosing to sacrifice what you want at the moment for what you want most is to clarify what you really want. After you've identified what you really want, the most important question you can ask yourself is, how bad do I really want it? That is the question that determines everything. Because if you want something bad enough, you will do whatever it takes to have it. Including sacrificing to get it. If not, you will just keep talking about what you want and putting no real action behind it. There has to be a time when you embrace that nothing of significance can be accomplished without some serious sacrifices. The sooner that you accept that truth is when things will become very black and white for you. At that moment, you will be forced to be honest with yourself, and it will become evident if you really want what you say you want because your actions will clearly demonstrate what you want most. Your actions will speak far louder than your mouth ever will. And if you are serious about doing the things that you say you want to do, you will slowly start giving things up that hinder you and start moving towards your goals.

ELIMINATING DISTRACTIONS

The closer you get to your goals, and the more you accomplish, you will begin to move with a new clarity and the things that once held value would no longer hold the value they did. You will start to see clearly how the things that you allowed to distract you were enemies to your destiny and could come before your dreams. Often times when we are consumed enjoying whatever it is that we are enjoying, we don't realize what we are giving up in the process because we are too busy enjoying life. In order to move expediently towards your dreams, you have to eliminate any and all distractions because distractions will do one of two things, either they will kill your dreams or prolong you getting to your destination. And getting to your destination past the season that you were supposed to arrive, could result in you missing that opportunity. I had to be honest with myself about all the things that were holding me back because choosing to be willfully in denial about the areas that were holding me back were some things that were hard, to be honest about. But it had to be done because I was tired of staying stuck in place only making minimal progress. It was hard to admit that the amount of time I was investing in things that didn't serve me were distractions. It was hard to realize that TV was standing in the way of me and my destiny. And even harder to accept that although I was on social media for brand building that it was consuming too much of my time. These were things that I enjoyed immensely, but there is no way that I would enjoy them more than the satisfaction of getting to my life's goal. There will always be time to watch tv or surf the web, but my dream may not always be before me. Like I told you before, there is a window of opportunity associated with some goals and dreams, and when the window is up, you've missed that opportunity. The truth of the matter is, if I were unwilling to sacrifice the things that I mentioned, I wouldn't have even been able to write this book. So after really realizing that it was either my goals or the things that I was distracted by, the decision became easier to give up those things for the things that I want most.

COMMIT TO IT

The prerequisite to start moving towards your goals is making a commitment that no matter what, you will remove anything, I mean ANYTHING that threatens to stand in the way of you and your goals out of your life. I don't care what or who it is. It is literally that serious. When I made that decision, I was so serious about it that it didn't matter if it was my mother standing in the way of my dreams, she would have had to go. Of course, I'm facetious, but there is a degree of truth to it. I am not opposed to removing anybody or anything out of my way when it comes to getting where I want to go in my life. When you get to this place, you will be unstoppable. You will be able to move forward with a laser focus unrestricted by distractions and things that can hold you back. You will be off and running, and your accomplishments will begin to pile up because you will be in a place where you can focus all of your mental energy on your goals. As long as you stay committed to sacrifice whatever is necessary to get to your goals, you will eventually get there. Whenever you find yourself getting off track and allowing distractions to come in, as soon as you identify them, eliminate them and get back on course. Don't beat yourself up about them, just simply identify them, eliminate them, and get back focused.

But with all of this hard work, there must be some balance in your life. As important as it is to work with a laser focus, it is equally important to have some leisure time to do things that allow you time to debrief. When I suggested eliminating distractions, I wasn't suggesting that you should never get on social media or watch television or whatever it is that you do for enjoyment, that would be unreal. I was simply suggesting that you prioritize the important things to take precedence over everything else. I strongly recommend making a schedule or designating time for those things in a way that it does not interfere with what you need to be doing to obtain your goals. It's important to be disciplined when you create this schedule so that you can find time to get your work done as well as do the things that you enjoy without any guilt. Having a healthy work-life balance is paramount to not burning out, so make sure you remember to incorporate some leisure time.

Always keep in mind that success will always require something of you. Is it easy to give up the things that you enjoy to have what you want in the future? The answer is emphatically NO! But after all, what you want most has to be the focal point to help you make the decision that is most conducive to your future. As long as you keep your eyes on the long-term goals versus what's in front of you now, you will position yourself to make a decision that could impact the next 20-30 years of your life.

Your life will never be what it could be if you spend your entire life giving in to temporary pleasures. Only the hard work of sustaining a disciplined life where you deny yourself now for what you want in the long run will produce the results that you want and move you closer to your dreams.

Always weigh out what is really important to you, do your best to eliminate every distraction and commit to doing whatever it takes to remove any obstacle standing in the way of you getting to your destiny. Your future will thank you for it, and your sacrifices will yield a return if you deny yourself the pleasures of today for the fulfillment of tomorrow.

CHAPTER 9
YOUR BIGGEST INVESTMENT

"The best investment you can make is in yourself."

—Warren Buffett

Investing in yourself is the single most important investment you will ever make in your life. While investing in things like real estate, stocks, and bonds play a huge role in you becoming successful, investing in yourself outweighs them all. The investment in self is the foundation upon which all other areas will benefit from. It is the baseline where you acquire the education and knowledge to apply towards whatever endeavors you choose to pursue. In most fields, the top earners are usually those with the most knowledge. When you invest in yourself, you build up knowledge which will benefit you as you go after your goals. When you begin to build anything, it is important to start by building on a solid foundation. Investing in self is the most solid foundation that you can build for your future.

A lot of people don't invest in themselves for a couple of different reasons, either they don't see how investing in themselves right now will help them in the immediate future, or they feel like they don't have the resources to invest in themselves. A lot of people that are struggling financially living paycheck to paycheck feel like, "I can't afford to invest in myself." When the truth of the matter is that they can't afford not to. When you are not where you want to be and barely making ends meet, the only way to get out of that situation is by doing something to increase your earning power. The more of a skill set that you have, or the more knowledge you have in a particular field, the more you increase your earning ability. But if you sit back and allow business to be done as usual and do nothing to improve upon that which you are, you will never increase your earning power.

Don't get me wrong; I'm not saying that if you invest in yourself today, you will immediately start seeing results tomorrow, although you could. When you invest in building on your knowledge what usually happens is that the results are not instantaneous, but over the course of time you acquire enough knowledge to become really good at what you do. And when you become really good at what you do, people will pay you for what you do. When you decide to invest in yourself, you have to go in seeing the BIG picture; you can't go in short-sighted looking for instant results. You have to be certain that what you invest in yourself will pay off in the long run. It may take some time, but one thing is for sure, whenever you take the time to invest in yourself, there is always a return on investment; always, which is why you have to be patient. Look at it this way, you have your whole life to live, and the work that you do on yourself today will benefit you tomorrow.

INCREASING YOUR STOCK

There are so many benefits to investing in your personal development that it's hard to fathom why anybody wouldn't do so. The most important benefit is the person you become in the process. I can't even begin to express how much my life has changed as I have begun to invest in my development. My mind has grown by leaps and bounds, and my confidence has grown exponentially the more and more that I have invested in myself. I have created a brand-new lifestyle for myself that is a far cry from my upbringings just by making the investment of feeding my mind on a continual basis with techniques and strategies on how to become better at what I do. I have been able to tap into the minds of some of the most influential men and women in the world just by seeking out the information. I'm talking about the likes of Les Brown, Zig Ziglar, Jim Rohn, and Warren Buffett to name a few. And most of it didn't cost me anything at all; I had to simply seek it out. There is so much information out there readily available on the internet waiting that's just a click away. But, most people never take the time to access what's available to them. And as a result, they stay stuck in the same place year after year complaining, never moving forward because they never took the time to invest in themselves. Nothing becomes better without working on it. Anything you do in life you have to be intentional about becoming better. You have to be constantly working on your craft, the moment that you get comfortable and think you are fine where you are, you have already lost.

I want to share the story of three entrepreneurs that decided to go into business together fresh out of college. All throughout college, they had a pact with each other that they would save all the spare money that they had so that when they got out of college, they would start a landscaping business. So, all throughout college, they worked odd jobs and saved every dime they could so that they could invest in their business. As graduation approached, they were all excited that they were close to graduating and starting their own business. They had all accumulated about ten thousand dollars seed money to start their business, and they are all ready to go. The weekend before graduation, they all decided to go to Las Vegas. They thought why not we've all worked hard for the last four years let's go out and celebrate. So, they did what most young people do in Vegas when they are celebrating, they lived it up! They went to parties, they caught some of the shows and even did a little gambling. Two of the three guys only brought the money that they had saved for the trip, but the third friend thought I'll bring two thousand dollars just to be on the safe side. So, he went to the blackjack table initially just planning on playing with a hundred dollars. But before he knew it he was down five hundred dollars. Oh, but wait there's a catch, did I mention the money that he was playing with was money from the savings that he was supposed to have to start the business? He thought I could never tell my friends about what happened; they would kill me. So, he decided to try to play until he got his money back. Over the next 2 hours, he exhausted the entire two thousand dollars. At this point, he began to panic and called home for more money; before he knew it, he had lost a whopping five thousand dollars. At this point, he felt defeated and figured, hey I might as well get another thousand to try to get my money back. After another couple of hours of gambling, he lost a total of eight thousand dollars. The next morning, he told his friends what happened, and they were devastated. Their thirty-thousand-dollar seed money was now twenty-two thousand dollars. As you can imagine, they were very disappointed. Even though they were disappointed, they allowed the third friend to invest his two thousand dollars in the company. Although they let him invest, his deficit left the company in a compromised position struggling to obtain equipment that they would have had the resources to get.

After a rough couple of years, the landscaping company started to take off. They started to see a couple hundred-thousand-dollar profit per year. My question is, do you think the friend that invested two thousand should reap the same amount of profit as the other two friends?

I'm sure many of you are saying NO because he didn't invest what they invested. Well, if that is the case, then if you are not investing the time, energy, and resources that the successful people are investing, what makes you think you should reap the same reward as them? The moral of the story is this; you should never expect a return where you are not willing to invest.

TAKING THE PLUNGE

I want to ask you to consider a very important question. What will happen if you never decide to invest in yourself? Who will be impacted by your decision not to? And are you willing to endure having a fraction of the life that you could've had if you just took the time to invest in yourself? I was just talking to my personal trainer today and commending him on the growth that I see in his online marketing. The difference in his marketing is night and day from just two weeks ago. I asked him what the difference was. He told me he hired a fitness marketing coach. I could immediately see the impact that the marketing coach had on him in just a few weeks. Now imagine if this man who is pretty successful by his own right didn't see the value in hiring somebody with more knowledge than him to help him get to where he is trying to go. What could the consequence have been? The information that he has that he is now applying to his business he wouldn't have had. And who knows what kind of impact that would have had on his business. Coaches hire coaches because they understand that the fastest way to reduce the learning curve and get to where you want to get to is by learning from somebody that is well versed in that area. Small investments of time, energy, and resources can lead to big rewards; you have to see the value of your investment.

A RETURN ON YOUR INVESTMENT

How can one start the process of investing in themselves? That's the million-dollar question. It's not as complicated as one might think. The answer to the question is just to start where you are. Do you want to know who my number one mentor is? Google and YouTube. Anything that you want to learn is at your fingertips. Any information that you want to learn about any subject you can find by looking at those two sources. I am the farthest from tech-savvy, but just by accessing YouTube, I was able to learn how to edit videos for my weekly YouTube show just by searching for the information. So, I would say, start with the resources that you have. You may not have the money to invest in yourself right now. But start with what you have, YouTube and Google are your best friend. Start with the resources that you have available to you. If you have the resources to invest in yourself, strongly consider doing so. Trust me when I say that there will be a return on your investment. I would like to provide you with some practical tips on how you can invest in yourself.

1. **Start Where You Are** - Like I mentioned in the above paragraph, simply start where you are and begin to invest in yourself with what's available to you. Only you know what resources are available to you. Take the time to evaluate what options that you have and begin to invest in whatever ways you can. What books can you read? What podcasts are available on the information that you aspire to obtain? What workshops or seminars are within your budget that you could attend? These are just a few of the questions that I would ask you to ask yourself as you begin to think about investing your time, energy, and resources into yourself.

2. **Sacrifice To Invest** - When you really begin to understand how important to invest in yourself is, you will find a way to sacrifice. I was reading a book by Brian Tracy that really emphasized saving at least 3% of your annual income to work on self-improvement and becoming consistently better. He told the story of a young employee in sales that was just beginning in their career. This particular employee was a little different from the rest as he was really determined to become successful in the world of sales. So he set out to become one of the best. He began watching what all the other successful people in sales did and began to mock them. Like all the other new employees to sales were lackadaisical about becoming really proficient in sales, he was the exact opposite. They would come in either right at the start of their shift or late, he was there early. Unlike the other employees, he would stay late putting in as much effort as he could to become more efficient with what he did, at the end of their shifts they would be running out of the door. They rarely did anything to improve their skill set to develop but he started reading every book on sales and attended every seminar that he could to increase his knowledge of sales and what ended up happening was mind-blowing. Month by month his sales began to increase based on the knowledge that he acquired. As he was once

one of the regular salespeople, within six months, he became one of the top salesmen in the company. What was the difference between him and the rest of the team that he started with? He took the time to invest in himself and his knowledge and that information paid off for him ten times over. So my suggestion to you my friend is to look at the areas of your life where you may be able to cut back on the resources to invest in yourself. The three-day workshop that I went to that taught me the very techniques to write this book cost me thirty-six dollars. The information that I learned in that workshop is allowing me to fulfill one of my lifelong dreams. It all started with a desire to invest in myself to become more knowledgeable in an area that I thought would benefit me. Only God knows the rewards that will come from that investment. But let's just hope they are plentiful.

3. **Read, Read, Read** - I can't tell you how much knowledge that I have acquired through reading. Like I mentioned earlier in this chapter, there is no way possible for you to have all of the knowledge that is out there, but you don't have to. Reading allows you to tap into some of the most influential minds that have ever lived. To have access to the thoughts and ideas of some of the progressive thinkers is a blessing. Just like you are reading this book right now, you are not only tapping into my personal thoughts and ideologies but those of everybody that has influenced me over my 40 years of living. So, no matter what you do, take the time to read. It sharpens your mind and gives you access to information that could change your life. It's all about mindset development. Les Brown says that the best way to interrupt the negative thoughts that tend to race through our mind is by replacing them with positive, uplifting content. The best way to do so is reading.

4. **Events** - Do not, I repeat, do not be afraid to invest in going to workshops and seminars. I know sometimes they feel gimmicky and like they are just out to sell you a product, and the truth of the matter is they are. But what I need you to ask yourself is, what is the value of the product? If you were to spend 5k on a product that would net you a 25k profit over the next year would it be worth it? Or would you be hung up on spending the 5k? The successful people understand that to make money, you must spend money. Don't get so caught up in the spending that you don't factor in what you could receive by constantly working to improve yourself. In one seminar that I went to last year, I heard from 8 speakers that all offered a varying skill set. But every one of them offered something of value. While I wasn't able to invest in every one of their programs, I invested in what was most valuable to me at the time, that was the book writing seminar. And the skill set that I learned there has proved to be valuable as I near the completion of this book. The irony of it all is that the initial seminar that I invested my time in because it didn't cost me any money exposed me to the book writing seminar. Where you invest your time and resources is important.

5. **Hire A Coach** - I cannot begin to express how important coaches are. Not because I am a Life Coach, but because I truly understand the important role that coaches play in people's development. It's crazy how we realize this in some areas of life but do not recognize the need in other areas of life. For instance, when people are looking to lose weight or become fit, there is not a lot of frets when it comes to hiring someone that is more knowledgeable. The first thing they think of is hiring a personal trainer. However, imagine someone that is struggling with their fitness goals, that does not know proper nutrition and has no idea of what machine is for what when they go to the gym. What do you think their progress will be like if any? Now imagine that same person getting a customized meal plan that

factors in their weight, height, activity level, and fitness goals from a person that has spent years studying nutrition to help people. Imagine that same trainer giving them a customized workout plan to address the fitness piece. Imagine the difference in the results. That's what a coach does for you. A personal trainer is merely a coach with a different title. If people understand that as it relates to fitness, why is there such a disconnect with people seeing their need for a coach as it relates to their personal and professional needs outside of fitness? In any area of your life where you are not achieving the results that you aspire to achieve, it may be time to look at a coach. I recently sought out a therapist, not because I have any special needs, but simply because I want to be as emotionally healthy as I can possibly be. She was able to expose me to some areas of myself that I did not see. She was also able to suggest some strategies to address areas of my life that I desired to grow. The moral of the story is, don't be afraid to get support in growing in areas of your life that require growth, and a coach just may be the person to assist you in doing that. There are fitness coaches, finance coaches, coaches that deal with emotional and spiritual needs, etc., there is a coach for just about anything. If there is an area of your life that you have struggled with progressing on your own and you desire to, I will support you with considering hiring a coach.

I can't begin to emphasize how important investing in yourself is. Hopefully, this chapter has gotten you to think about the ways that you could benefit from investing in yourself. The whole focus of investing in yourself is about mindset development and intentional constant improvement. The time you take to develop yourself now will benefit you in the long run. The results may not be apparent right away, but you will see them in the long run. There is no way for a person to work on themselves on a consistent basis and not see results. The more that you increase your knowledge and skill set, the more valuable you become. The real question becomes, are you important enough for you to invest in yourself and your future? Are you willing to endure the consequences of not doing so?

I would like to propose a challenge to you. Over the next 30 days, I would like to ask you to spend one hour each day filling your mind with motivational, spiritual, or knowledge-based content for simply increasing your knowledge. At the end of the challenge, I want to ask you to submit your testimonies to info@edwardlmoore.com to let me know how you feel and what changed for you after engaging in a month of investing in yourself. Happy investing and I hope to hear from you all in a month.

CHAPTER 10
FINDING YOUR NICHE

"If you do what you love you'll never work another day in your life"

—Marc Anthony

Many of you may be saying, "I have read the book, I've digested the content, I even agree with it, but there is just one BIG problem." "I don't know what to do with it." "I don't know what my purpose or my calling is." "I don't know what my niche is." "I have no idea of what I want to do." "I now have all of this good information, but I don't know what to apply it towards." "What should I be doing?" "What are my next steps?" That is a question that many people struggle with; they simply don't know what direction to go in to create the life that they want for themselves. They feel completely stuck, feeling like the uncertainty that they struggle with is about to strangle the life out of them. While this feeling can feel never-ending, trust me there is hope.

The creator made every living individual with unique talents and gifts. There is not one individual alive that was not born with some gifting. When you were created, there was nothing special that you did to earn them, you were simply born with them. I can say with all certainty that there is something that you do well that you excel at that is specific to you. You may not be aware of what that is or may not be currently using it, but that does not mean it's not there. The problem is this; some so many people have gifts lying dormant inside of them that don't have any clue on how to identify what they are. Through my journey of struggling to identify what my gift was, I've come to understand that the gifts are always there. We just don't always recognize them for what they are. I didn't start to become aware of what my giftings were until I invested some time into taking inventory to find out what I was good at. Many people never even take the time to study themselves to find out what they excel at and, yet they run through life complaining that they don't know what they should be doing that would give them fulfillment and provide them with the means to live the type of life they desire. When attempting to find your "niche," it is important that you begin to examine who you are and what makes you unique and stand out from the crowd. It's equally important to take notice of the things that you have been complimented on regularly and do well naturally. The reason for that is because you have to begin to see those things as gifts. If you just see yourself as just another average person with no talents or special abilities, you may very well overlook the very thing that sets you apart.

As I look back over my own life to where I am now, it is easy to identify the gifts that were lying dormant inside of me. Growing up like most kids in urban neighborhoods, I wanted to be a professional athlete or entertainer. Never in my wildest dreams did I see myself becoming an Inspirational Speaker, let alone a Life Coach coming from the dysfunctional lifestyle that I came from. But as I look back with clarity, I see that the gifts that I operate in now were always there. I remember being young and having the ability to influence other people to follow me before I even knew what it was. I also remember speaking passionately about things and people gravitating to what I was saying long before the thought of being a speaker popped into my mind. I guess the point that I am trying to drive home here is that you have gifts. You just have to find them. Once you find out what you are good at and what you are passionate about, it will answer the questions that you have been looking for in relation to what you should be doing with your life. Everybody has their own lane, something that is specific to you. Once you find out what that is, your life will change forever.

THE VALUE OF FINDING YOUR GIFT

Are you tired of the current state of your life? Do you feel there is more for you? Are you currently unfulfilled doing what you are doing professionally? Are you doing what you need to do to pay the bills but not something you're passionate about? If you answered yes to any of these questions, it's time for some change. Imagine getting to the end of your life only having done what you thought you needed to do to provide, never tapping into the gifts in you that could have changed your entire life. Your gifts were not just given to you to meet the needs of others; they were also given to you for your benefit as well. Imagine not only doing something that you are passionate about but being able to provide a living for yourself doing what you love as well. There is a way to monetize your gifts. The more that you develop your gift to provide value to others, the more marketable it becomes. In this day and age, you can build a business from almost anything. If you market it correctly, you could benefit from it. I've had the pleasure of seeing some of the most uncommon things take off because there is a market for everything.

Any gift that you could possibly provide, there is someone that needs and would pay for that service. You just have to get that gift in front of the right people; people that will appreciate it as well as see the value in it. Where you begin to build your real value at is by being authentic to who you are. There is not another soul in the world that can do what you do in the same exact way that you do it which holds value in itself. There is a value to being authentic and doing what you were born to do because in doing so you begin to set yourself apart. The more that you set yourself apart, you begin to create a lane that's specific to you. Have you ever noticed how the people that are true to themselves seem to stand out and draw the attention of other people? That comes from being true to one's own self and following the course that's best suited for you. That has never been more noticeable than in music. The people that are being true to who they are and giving you their authentic selves; music seems to draw you in ways that those that follow the crowd never could. It is utterly important to figure out who you are so that you can do what works for you. Never get caught up in trying to determine what you should be doing by watching others always keep the focus on self-knowing that your lane is specific to you.

So many people do things because they see other people doing those things only to get into those professions and hate them because they attempted to do what they saw others become successful at. They don't realize that the person they mimicked may be walking in their gift and doing something that they have a passion for.

I remember wanting to go into real estate because I saw one of my childhood friends become very successful at it, without ever giving questioning, is this something that agrees with my skill set or something I have a passion for? The worst thing that you could ever do is to pursue something just because you saw somebody else become successful at it. So many people go into careers just for the money and end up miserable because they end up doing something that they either are not good at or do not have a passion for. I'm glad I had the wherewithal to understand that it was more important for me to pour my energy into where my passion was and something that I am naturally skilled at.

That's why I decided to become a speaker. Whenever I invest time and energy towards my current goals which are in alignment with my purpose, it never feels like work. Is it challenging? Yes. Is it hard work? Yes. But it never feels like a chore because it's something that I'm passionate about.

When you find your niche, you will begin to establish yourself as a specialist in your field. That's why it's imperative to be very specific about what it is that you want to do because when you get good at what you do, you will be sought out for your skillset. Let me give you an example. Let's say you were having back problems that wouldn't go away if you had the option to go to a general practitioner or a chiropractor, who would you choose? Of course, you would choose the chiropractor. Why? Because the chiropractor specializes in your problem. Consumers are the same way, if you offer a product or service that specializes in what they need, they will come to you for it. The more you develop that gift to provide product or service, the more you set yourself apart from everybody else without specialized services. Look at my brand, for example, I have coined myself "Mr. No Excuses," so anybody that is looking to grow and eliminate excuses from their life will come looking for the guy that has dedicated his life to creating strategies to eliminate excuses. People are always willing to pay for solutions to their problems. So, if your gift can help others or provide a service for them even if it's entertainment, you can monetize it.

THE SEARCH FOR YOUR GIFT

What problems does your gift solve? Does your gift meet the need of people? Does it provide a service? Or does it simply make people feel good? Not every gift is a tangible product. Think about the gift of a musician, the gift that they possess holds value. It provides a service for people and makes them feel good. Imagine going through life without music. I don't even want to try to imagine that. Our gift is the thing that we should be spending the most time developing as it is what we were purposed to do. The problem is, we get so consumed doing what we feel we need to do to provide that our gift takes the back burner. Imagine if in high school everybody was taught how to identify their gift, was then taught how to nurture their gift, then taught a plan of how they could monetize their gift by the time they left high school? Can you imagine how many more people would be happy and successful?

What are some of the things that you have excelled at in the past? What are some of the things that you do well naturally? If you don't know what they are, it may be time to do some exploration. Your gift is just waiting to be uncovered, but you must do the work to unearth it. I want you to take a second to think about what lane would you create for yourself in a perfect world? What would you be doing? What would your life look like? I want you to understand that the best life that you envision for yourself is totally achievable. It takes some very intentional work of developing yourself and your gift but nonetheless achievable. The last question that I'm going to ask you is probably the most important one in this whole chapter, what is your plan to identify what your gift is? I want you to think about a strategy to uncovering your gift really. To jump-start you in the process, I would like to provide you with some tangible tips to support you in the process.

FINDING YOUR NICHE

Finding your gift or your niche as the world calls it can be a challenging process if you don't know where to start. In this portion of the chapter, I want to provide you with some practical tips that have allowed me to identify my gift so that I could start the process of developing it, to ultimately monetizing it. The first thing that you need to understand is that when you create a product or service, is that it cannot be strictly for monetary gain. Whenever you lead with making sure the needs of your consumer is met and make the need of the customer priority, financial gain will always follow. So always start there. The formula is always people first, profit second and always, I mean always be looking to add value to who you serve.

INVENTORY CHECK

Alright, let's explore some ways that you can begin to uncover your gifts. The first place that I would start is by taking an inventory of everything that you are good at. Get a notebook and write down everything that you have excelled at over the course of your life. I'm talking about the things that you do well naturally. Things that you do effortlessly as well as come easily to you. A lot of times, we have gifts sitting right under our nose, and we don't even realize it because we've never taken the time to be intentional about examining what we do well.

UNCOVERING YOUR PASSION

The next thing that I want you to do on that same list is to write down all the things that you are passionate about. What gets your fire going? What things are you naturally just drawn to and you don't know why? The things that you are passionate about are key indicators to areas where your niche may reside at. Let me give you an example. I am very drawn to tv shows like Lockup MSNBC. I didn't know why, but any television show that has something to do with jail, I just love it. However, that doesn't happen by chance. I really did some introspective work and asked myself, why are you so drawn to jail shows so much? I realized that the reason that I'm so drawn to them is because that is where part of my life's work is. I examined all of the jobs that I had since I have worked in the social service sector and I realized that out of all the jobs that I had, I felt the most fulfilled when I worked inside the jail. Part of my purpose is working with individuals that have been incarcerated and desire to turn their lives around. I used this as an example to show that the things that you're are passionate about hold some significance; that is also a part of my work that is very specific to me. This is one of my areas of concentration "my niche" if you will. They say that somewhere between your passion and your purpose you will find your gift, so keep looking.

NARROWING YOUR FOCUS

It's important to narrow your focus and get very specific about what area of concentration that you want to focus on so that you can invest all of your energy into that particular area. I have a good friend of mines that is also a life coach, somebody that I have worked with over the course of the past few years. He wanted to take his brand to the next level. I was continuously suggesting, "You have to find your niche." He was never really able to take his brand to the next level because he didn't have an area of concentration. Being a coach is broad. But what was his area of specialty? One day last week, I shared some insight that I received from my higher power that I was instructed to share with him on what his niche was. He received it, and it provided him with clarity and direction. Since that day, he has begun to develop and design his coaching business with a specific focus. That has done a couple of things for him; it took away all the stress and worry associated with not knowing what direction to go in, the next thing it did was provide him with a roadmap on what to do based on being clear on his direction. My suggestion is the same to you, seek out clarity on a specific area of focus, the clarity will provide a roadmap to your destination for you.

FROM PASSION TO PROFIT

Lastly, if you want to figure out a way to monetize your gift, connect your gift to a service that people need. Look at my case, for example; my passion is speaking to people to motivate and inspire them. I would do it for free; I am just that passionate about it, I truly desire to help people. But there is a market for that. Any time that you can speak into people's lives and help them break through barriers and excel personally and professionally, there is a value to that. Never overlook the value that your gift has. As I mentioned earlier, your gift was not only given to you to be a blessing to others but to be a blessing to you also. What value does your gift bring to people? Every gift holds value, and after you do the work to find out what your gift is, begin to develop it so that it is refined, you can then monetize it as it will hold value to people.

So, if you are one of the many people that feel stuck like you don't know what to do, use the tips provided in this chapter as a starting point to help you begin to narrow down what your niche is. Always remember that every one of us has a unique gift and it is our job to figure out what that gift is. Who you see yourself as is an essential part of identifying your gift because you may be capable of doing extraordinary things. However, if you don't believe it, you won't see that as an option for you. Once you identify what your niche is, you will begin to set yourself apart from everybody else because you have a specific skill set that people will seek you out for.

Figuring out your gift is liberating because it will provide you with direction and clarity, and the sense of confusion and being stuck will be alleviated because you now have a focus to direct your energy towards. So that's where the work has to start. You have to identify your gift so that you can develop it and ultimately monetize it. One thing I want you to remember is that once you begin to share your gift with the world, always prioritize being a blessing to who you serve with your gift; the money will come. Never do anything motivated purely by financial gain, always put the people first. And in closing, always do what's a good fit for you. There are a million things that make money, but you were created with a gift that is specific to you. My prayer is that you find it. Now go out there and find your "niche" and bless the world with it.

PART FOUR
ADAPTABILITY

CHAPTER II
THE ART OF BOUNCING BACK

"Success is not final, failure is not fatal: it is the courage to continue that counts."
—Winston Churchill

When I think of the word resiliency, I'm reminded of a story of a prizefighter that was engaged in a heavyweight bout. This particular fighter was a heavy underdog to lose the bout, and as expected he faced the challenge of a lifetime. He came out in the first round determined to give it all that he had and shock the world. As he came out, he circled the ring sizing up his opponent only to find out that his opponent was everything that urban legend had pegged him to be. By the time the first blow landed, he knew that he was in for a long night. Blow after blow; he struggled to maintain his balance and focus in an attempt to endure the menacing blows. Despite going against many people's advice to even take the fight, he was determined to give it his best shot. He figured, "What do I have to lose?" The way he saw it was, "They can measure our heights and weights, but what they can't measure is the amount of fight in our hearts." So, despite losing badly in the bout, he came out round after round determined to finish what he started. As it went into the later rounds, the abuse that he was taking became too much as he finally hit the canvas. The blow that sent him to the canvas was so vicious that nobody expected him to get up. As he stood back up to his feet, the referee administered a standing eight count. He looked him in the eyes and asked him are you ok?" He looked at the referee and said, "I'm ok! Let's go." As he touched gloves with his opponent, they squared back up in the middle of the ring. His opponent stalked him in the ring like a lion waiting in hunt for a gazelle. Every direction that he went in, his opponent walked him down. Moments later, his opponent hit him with a barrage of punches sending him back to the canvas again. The referee stepped in again sending both men to their respective corners. Although he is slow to get up, he somehow made his way to his corner. The referee came over to evaluate whether or not he thinks he can continue. His cornermen stepped in to also evaluate him to see whether or not he can continue. His cornermen asked him again almost pleading with him, "Man do you want to continue?" He looked his cornermen in the eyes and said, "No matter what happens, do not let him stop this fight!" Against their better judgment, they agreed to let him continue. The referee stepped in and did another eight count. He came out more determined than ever hell-bent on finishing this fight. By the opening of the next round, he was once again taking more and more punishment. By this time, the punishment was unbearable, and he was sent to the canvas with another crushing blow. At this point, the fight was totally a one-sided fight, and his corner was ready to throw in the towel. But to everybody's amazement, he bounced back up like a machine hell-bent on surviving this punishment.

When I think about resiliency, this is the image that comes to mind. Being resilient is about having the internal fortitude to be the type of individual that no matter what blows are dealt to you in life, you continue to find the will to get back up. Even when the odds are against you, and there is nothing that suggests that you will win, you fight the urge to give up because you know that as long as you are still in the fight, there is a chance for victory.

KEEP ON DIGGING

Resiliency is the ability to bounce back from things or situations that don't go as planned in our lives. We all need to be resilient because at some point we will all experience setbacks and challenges. Some of us are stronger than others. Anytime you go to do anything of significance you will be met with resistance. Nothing worth doing will come easy. You will inevitably experience challenges along the way, but you have to be strong enough to take the blows and keep on going. Life is full of challenges. Contrary to what many people think, success is not a straight path. Many successful people will tell you that they failed on their way to success. They experienced many setbacks before they actually arrived at their goal. In order to succeed in life, you have to have tough skin. You will have plans that will not go as you exactly planned, you will have people that reject your ideas and you may even go without the support of those that you think will support you, but you have to keep on going. This journey of arriving at our destiny is not a sprint, but more like a marathon, which means you have to be in for the long haul. You have to be determined that no matter what it looks like if you remain persistent, you will ultimately get to your goal. It reminds me of the meme that illustrates a man in a mine digging for diamonds with a pickaxe. The meme suggests that the man had spent a great deal of time digging for his treasure but ended up getting tired quitting and giving up just short of reaching his goal. The diamonds that he was searching for were just on the other side of that last dig. Had he kept on going just a little further, he would have gotten to his goal. How many times in life could we have potentially been one dig away from getting to our goals, but we stopped just short of success? You never know when your time will be or when your breakthrough will come which is why you have to keep going despite whatever is going on around you. Life is full of unexpected events, sometimes things will be going good, and other times you may be facing catastrophes, but nevertheless, you have to find the will to endure.

STAY IN THE FIGHT

I want you to think back for a second and think over your life. In what areas of your life have you had to be resilient? What have you endured and came out on top like a champion? Although we may not realize it, we all have had to be resilient at some point in our lives. Do you want to know how I know? It's because we have all faced problems. And some of the problems that we have faced have left us no options but to be resilient. The fact that you are still here right now reading this book suggests that you are an overcomer. My question to you is, how can you apply the resiliency that resides in you to every area of your life? How can you access that resiliency that's inside of you that you had no choice but to use when your circumstances left you no options?

The funny thing about life is this, sometimes you never really know just how much resilience you possess until you are put in a situation where you are forced to use it. Often times what stops us from tapping into the resiliency that resides on the inside of us is fear. Let me go a little bit deeper when faced with a big problem or challenge; it's easy for one to become fearful especially when it's something that you have never faced or have no control over the outcome. Fear is a paralyzing emotion and acts as an enemy of resiliency because fear keeps you stuck in place, while resiliency is about moving forward. Resilience is the belief that no matter what happens in my life, I will be ok and that I can bounce back from whatever comes my way. In life, everybody experiences challenges, but how you respond to them is what will determine whether you win or lose. If every time you're faced with a challenge you fold under pressure and just give in to your circumstance, you will never win. I'm not at all suggesting that life is not tough and that you will not go through some things that test your resolve, I'm simply suggesting that as long as you have breath in your lungs, there is nothing that you can't bounce back from.

Many people have asked me how I was able to bounce back from all that I have endured in my life. From experiencing the abandonment of my parents to being a high school dropout to overcoming all the mistakes that I made early in life to get where I am now. All I can say is, I never gave up. As many times as I wanted to quit, as many as times as I wanted to give up, and as many times that I felt that there was nothing to fight for, I just never gave up. I'm suggesting that you do the same thing. No matter what you go through in this life, don't give up! No matter what you go through, don't give in. And no matter what you go through, always remember that things can and will get better. Most valleys in our lives are just a season and after the storm comes the sun. You just have to stay in the fight long enough to experience it peek its head through the clouds.

My question to you is, what are some tools that you can develop that will allow you to bounce back no matter what you experience? How can you hang in the fight long enough to overcome whatever comes your way? Although I will provide some practical steps to address the questions listed above, the answer to all of these questions already resides inside of you. One thing that life coaching has taught me is that the answers that we seek are already inside of us. Before you move on to the next part of this chapter, I am requesting that you really take some time to really answer these questions presented to you in this chapter. These questions were intentional and were asked for the specific purpose of you digging deeper and pulling out the answers that already exist inside of you. Here is a recap of the questions presented in the chapter. I hope that you read them and do some introspective work to start the process of uncovering the answers to the questions that reside on the inside of you.

QUESTIONS

1. What areas of your life have you had to be resilient?
2. What have you endured and came out on top like a champion?
3. How can you apply the resiliency that is inside of you to every area of your life?
4. How can you tap into the resiliency that's inside of you?
5. What are some tools that you can develop that will allow you to bounce back no matter what you experience?

SURVIVING THE STORMS

Building resilience is a serious business and is essential for being an overcomer. I want to provide you with four practical steps that have helped me become more resilient both personally and professionally.

1. **Holding On To Hope** - In order to be resilient, you have to have hope that things can get better. Because when you feel there is no hope you have no reason to stay in the fight. It's just like the prize fighter that I mentioned earlier in the chapter, although all odds were against him and he was experiencing the beatdown of a lifetime, he knew that he stood a chance if he just stayed in the fight. Nine times out of ten, you will survive if you just stay in the fight. Life is unbearable when you have no hope. Even the Bible states that hope deferred makes the heart sick. When you give up hope, you may as well throw in the towel. But I promise you the first step to winning is just hanging on long enough to endure the blows coming at you. Once the blows subside, you can plot your strategy to win.

2. **Digging Down Deep** - Being resilient requires digging down deep to that place within you where your strength resides. It requires connecting with your authentic self so that you can tap into the ability to bounce back from anything that comes against you in this life. It has resided in you since before you were created. You were created on purpose with a purpose and everything that it would take to fulfill your purpose already inside of you including resilience. Somehow in life, we lose connection with our life force, which is where the knowledge of who we really are resides. Somehow, we have to make our way back home. It's like having a generator lying around your house that is full of power but unplugged. The generator possesses power but without being plugged in is useless. It's time to plug back into our power sources so that we can become empowered to live victorious lives.

3. **Assess The Options Available To You** - Once you have weathered the storm and made it through the difficult initial barrage of punches that the challenge presented, you can then take some time to breathe to assess what options are available to you. When you open up your mind to the possibilities that are available to you, it will surprise you how many options that you really have. As a man thinketh so is he; so, when you see yourself as not having many options, you close yourself off from the opportunities that are there. In my personal experience, it has been essential to seek clarity when looking for direction. Many people take many avenues to get clarity, but for me, it has been about connecting with my higher power where all of my wisdom and direction comes from. When I connect with my higher power, I connect with the source of unlimited wisdom. Whatever you do, maintain an optimistic mindset because doing so will free you up to look for the many options that are available for you to change your situation.

4. **Be Adaptable** - In order to be an overcomer, you have to be adaptable because one thing that is consistent in life is change. Things change all the time, and if we are not able to adapt, then we are not able to successfully transition with the changes that we will inevitably be faced with at some point. Life is about as unpredictable as Bay Area weather. In this life, we will experience sudden tragedies, relationships will fall apart, friends and family members will unexpectedly pass, but we have to remain adaptable in order to continue to move forward. The more flexible you are, the easier you will be able to transition to a place of change. That's not saying that you like the change or even agree with it. I'm simply suggesting that we exercise wisdom in knowing that fighting and resisting the change will not serve you in moving forward. Change is one of the hardest things in the world to embrace especially when you are not prepared for it. The first step is to accept and embrace change so

that you can figure out how to make it work for you. As challenging as this is, I guarantee you that if you begin to apply this mindset to everything that you face in life, you will move from an unproductive place of stagnation to a place of being able to adjust to the many challenges that await us in life.

In order to make it through the storms of life that will inevitably come your way, you have to be resilient. You need to have a bounce-back mentality and a determination never to give up. I promise you; I would never have been able to make it without this mentality. Some of the things that I have experienced would've broken the average person. From being the product of a drug-addicted mother to having a father that didn't claim me, to being a teenage father, my mom dying of AIDS; the list goes on and on and on. I can remember the times where I wanted to give up, where there was no foreseeable way for things to get better, where I felt like my life was a lost. The only thing that kept me going was holding on to the small glimmer of hope that maybe, just maybe that my life could get better if I held on. I can't even take credit for it because it was something that God placed in me which enabled me not to give up. I sit here with tears in my eyes right now as I reflect back on those times in my life. And I say with all conviction that if you don't give up, you can make it. You would be surprised where your life could be in a year if you just don't give up! There is too much riding on it. God is amazing, and he can transform your life into one you can barely recognize. I am living proof. I went from being lost, frustrated, and confused to having peace and clarity in my life. I went from using sex, drugs, and alcohol to fill the places of emptiness and void in my life to coaching others through those same situations. I went from a high school dropout and drug-addicted teenage father to an entrepreneur, motivational speaker, and life coach. Who would've ever thought it's possible? But you know what, I would've never become any of those things if I had given up when things looked bleak for me. This is why I am so passionate about others building up resilience because I've seen what happens when people give up and they stop believing. I've seen what happens in their lives when they accept that their lives won't get any better than their current circumstance. It can always get better, things can always improve, and that will only happen through being steadfast, digging down deep, holding onto hope that things can change, and being adaptable when it does.

CHAPTER 12
PROGRESS IS A PROCESS

"Slow progress is better than no progress."

—Unknown

The journey to success is a very unpredictable one. You just never know how things will play out. You can be working hard for years and nothing pops, then all of a sudden you get your shot and the floodgates of success open up for you. You just never know. But that's one of the hardest parts about pursuing your goals; finding the wherewithal to remain persistent even in the face of delayed accomplishments. Nothing of significance happens overnight, that is why it is so important to have faith and to trust the process. If you have lined up all of your ducks in a row and consistently work towards your goals, the chances are very likely that you will arrive there at some point. You have to have an inner knowing. You have to know that you know, that you know that it's coming. Even when it doesn't look like it, you have to be so convinced of it that nothing in the world would be able to persuade you otherwise. Anybody can believe in something when they can see it, but few rarely hold on to the dream when their reality looks nothing like the dream they envision. They give up and move on to do something else, giving up before they arrive at their destination.

Having gone through many processes to experience wins in my life, I have learned to embrace the process because it prepares you to maintain the victory. As I mentioned earlier in this book, the process is where you get made at. There are some things that you grow to understand when you have gone through the process of development that you would have not otherwise known. Let me give you an example. Have you ever been through anything in life that while you were going through it, you didn't like it? But once it was over, you were glad that you had been through it? That's what the process does for you. It builds your strength, your knowledge, and your character in ways nothing else can. Delayed blessings teach you patience, lack creates hunger, and failure creates endurance which are all vital qualities to have if you plan to do anything of significance. When you get to the other side of the process and arrive at your destination, you realize just how important the process was. I think the problem is how we view the process. Many people look at the process as long, uncomfortable, and unbearable, but when you begin to look for the things that you were supposed to learn, you can find value all throughout the experience. I no longer fight the process, I embrace it because I know that there is something to be learned. And the irony of it all is that when I'm ready, and I have learned what I need to learn, I get elevated to the next level every time it never fails.

DON'T RUSH THE PROCESS

Many people get weary during the process; they get caught up watching the scoreboard as one of my favorite Motivational Speakers Eric Thomas says. It is easy to want to achieve your goal so bad that you begin to get weary because it's taking longer than you expected. We are all guilty of it, as I am writing these very words, I have been trying to fight off the feeling of becoming too anxious, and wanting to expedite the process of making it to the next level as well. It is a natural desire to want to move to the next level especially when you have been working hard. There is nothing wrong with the desire in and of itself, but we have to be careful not to rush too fast and miss out on what we are supposed to learn in the process. When you rush the process without learning the steps that it teaches you, you end up ill-prepared. That's why it's important to trust the process! When you add trust, faith, and patience to the process, it allows you time to examine where you are in relation to where you want to be. When you get clarity about where you are, you will be better prepared to make decisions that are in your best interest. This is why it's even more important to be careful of the decisions that we make while waiting on your time because desperation will cause you to make some decisions that may ultimately affect you in the long run. Opportunities that may not necessarily be the best situation for you will present themselves, and if you are not careful, you will make decisions that will cost you down the road. That's why it's important to be led by something bigger than your feelings. I told you in the chapter, "Your Feelings Don't Matter" that feelings are unreliable compass. When you make decisions based solely on how you feel, often times you make decisions that are motivated by clouded judgment. That's why patience during the process is so important because it gives you time to make decisions based on the wisdom that you have acquired as a result of going through the process. In order to avoid the pitfalls that come from making decisions in haste, we have to make sound decisions from a place of clarity, not just desire. Self-assessment is a huge part of understanding where you are in the process. To understand where you are in any process is priceless. There are some opportunities that you may want that you are not even ready for yet, and if you got them and performed poorly, you could affect your credibility as well as future opportunities. Self-assessment allows you to have an understanding of where you are and what areas you need to develop to get where you want to go. We all want to get to our goals, and we all want to become successful, but not everybody wants to go through the process that's required to get there.

Many people have a false perception of what success is. Success is not always measured by dollars and cents; society tells us that we are not successful unless we are reaping monetary rewards. I beg to differ. Success happens long before the money arrives. You are successful any time that you set a goal and start moving progressively towards it. You may not have fully reaped the benefits yet, but that does not mean that you are not on the path to success. And even being on the path is something to be recognized. Never allow your level of success to be dictated by the number of zeros in your bank account. Let's be real, money is important, and when you run a business the goal is always to profit, but money is not the only measure of success in life. I've learned that being successful is more about the person that you become during the process of dream chasing than the actual money because the person that you develop into will attract what you desire to you anyway. You know how some people seem like no matter what they do, they are successful. There is something that they possess internally that just draws what they desire most to them. So, can it be with all of us if we spend our time focusing on becoming the best version of ourselves in every area of our lives? The money will come as a byproduct. So, with that being said, be anxious for nothing, take time to develop and enjoy the journey of self-discovery and self-mastery. Your time will come, but don't be so focused on the perceived blessings of the future that you don't take time to enjoy the ones that are all around you in the present.

IN THE MEANTIME

Rather than clock-watching, I want to encourage you to focus on developing yourself and your gift in the interim. I think it's important for us to shift our thinking from trying to predict and anticipate when our breakthrough will come, to what we can do in the meantime to prepare for the opportunity when it comes. My question to you is, what can you do to develop yourself to be prepared when your time comes? What would that look like for you? Only you know what that looks like. What areas of your life need some work to prepare you for the great things that are inevitably coming your way?

If I can be all the way transparent to you, I have had to address several areas of my life to prepare for what awaits me. I had to work on not only my physical gift of speaking, but some more internal things like my work ethic, character, and integrity, because not addressing those things could have caused me to forfeit my dreams. Not only is it important to me, to be a living example of what I encourage others to do, but it is of utmost importance for me to be everything that I profess to be. I had to be brutally honest with myself. So many people think it's just about the gift, but it's not, it's about every part of you. It's about the internal person that you are left with when nobody else is around. Who is that person? In what ways does that person need to develop? It is important to start with the internal personal because that is who really determines how high you will soar. The reason that most people find themselves struggling to get to the next level is due to some internal barriers. Equally, those that experience great heights and end up falling is usually related to an internal issue of morality and integrity as well. It's important for your character to be in alignment with where you want to go. There is a saying that says, your gift will take you places that your character can't keep you. What part of the 'inner you' needs some work? Be honest with yourself and do some real introspective work, it will serve you well in the long run. To work on the external before working on the internal is putting the cart before the horse. The ultimate goal is to be fully prepared to walk into your destiny when that time comes, and the preparation always starts with self.

Lastly, after taking an honest assessment of what aspects of your internal self that needs some work, what part of your gift needs developing? Whatever your niche or gifting is, you must be committed to continuously bettering it. There is no cap, there is no ceiling, and you can always become better. The person that thinks their gift is fully developed and needs no development is misleading himself. There is no such thing as perfection as you can continue to improve daily. Self-mastery is a lifelong journey that one must be committed to until you take your last breath. In what ways can you begin to improve on your gift to make sure that it's polished and ready when the opportunity arrives? Trust me when I tell you if you start to ask yourself these questions and answer them thoughtfully and truthfully, and then begin to act upon the answers, there is no limit to how high you can soar.

In addition to the questions that I have just posed, I would also like to ask you a question that may be the most important of them all. When you are going through the process, and it doesn't look like you are going to get your breakthrough, and the dream just may not come true, what can you do to stay encouraged? If history has been an example of things to come, most successful people will tell you that there were times when they thought they were wasting their time and that their dream would never come to fruition, but they held on. They held onto the hope that despite what it looked like that what they aspired to do was possible. What can you do to encourage yourself in that type of way?

Who do you have around you that can encourage you when you feel like giving up? What is one thing that you can hold on to, to not throw in the towel when the going gets tough? It's not going to be easy by any stretch of the imagination, but you possess everything that it takes to make it. All you have to do is hold on long enough to see it come to fruition and trust the process.

PREPARE FOR YOUR SHOT

CHANGING YOUR MINDSET

As you wait for your circumstances to change, the very first thing that you have to do is to change your mindset around how you see the situation. You have to condition yourself to see the situation for what it really is. Not a situation where I'm going through this long drawn out process that feels like torture, but a process that is actually to my benefit, one that is preparing me for my next level. It is important to hold on to that truth because your circumstance will begin to speak to you louder than what you know to be true and cause you to accept false truths about your future. It is imperative that when thoughts of doubt, fear, and worry creep in that, you remind yourself of what you know to be true even though you can't see it. How you feel will often conflict with the truth, so it is important that you protect your mind and fill it with content that will reaffirm the truth. As a man thinks so is he, so it is your responsibility to protect the quality of your mind. Your mind is the vehicle that will navigate you where you want to go, so it is vital that it is always filled with the truth.

GET BUSY WORKING ON YOU

There are two ways that you can spend your time while waiting to get to your next level. The first is to wait in a place of anxiety anticipating every second, minute, and hour until you arrive at your destination. And the second is to put your head down and get busy to prepare for the future you want. The choice is yours. So many people spend their precious time focusing on what they have no control over instead of using that time wisely. What you do have control over is what you do with your time to prepare for when your number is called. I'm thankful for the time in between the wait and the fulfillment of some of my goals. I have learned so much to prepare that if I had not discovered what I have, I would have blown some major opportunities that I was not ready for. There is so much work to be done. My encouragement to you is to spend every waking moment that you have researching, learning, and developing yourself. Time will come when you will be called from behind the curtain and onto the stage and how well you perform will be based on how well you have prepared for that opportunity. So get lost in the work of developing yourself.

CELEBRATE THE SMALL WINS

As you travel down the road of success, you will experience several small wins before you get to the big one. Celebrate everyone because several small wins add up to the big one in the long run. Small wins build momentum and can aid you in staying encouraged as they represent faith that the big one is coming. It's like building blocks, after each win, you build on that victory, then the next one, and before you know it, your trajectory is one of progress. I get excited about every win, some that other people would look at as small or not significant enough to be excited about, but this is my experience. Whenever

I accomplish something no matter how small it is, it does something for me because I know that with that small accomplishment I have become one step closer to my ultimate goal. My encouragement to you is to do the same thing. Celebrate each and everything that you accomplish along your journey because every win is significant.

ALWAYS SELF ASSESS WHERE YOU ARE IN THE PROCESS

Now, this is one of the most important things that you can do as you work towards your goals. Know where you are! So many people suffer from illusions of grandeur and think they are at a level that they are not. When you understand where you are, it takes away from the anxiety of wanting to elevate before your time because you understand the work that you need to do to get to the next level. Self-assessment is one of the most valuable tools that a person can have because it keeps you in a place of reality versus thinking that you are entitled to something that you are not prepared to receive. Always assess where you are in any situation, and if you are not quite sure, ask for feedback. The last thing you want to do is thinking you are out here operating in excellence when you are mediocre at best. Feedback from people that love us enough to be honest with us over stroking our ego is priceless. That can be the difference between getting on stage looking like a fool and walking in excellence. Always be open to ways that you can improve and always make every attempt to do so.

TRUST THE PROCESS

Trusting the process requires having faith as well as having vision. It means being able to forecast and believing in something that you cannot physically see with your eyes, but know is coming. It is the understanding that in order to build anything you must do it in steps. First, you start by building a foundation, then the framing, and then ultimately the internal structure of your goals and dreams. When you understand the process, you understand that a long road of hard work is ahead of you, but that it is necessary to get where you are going. You understand that there's no time limit or magic time when you will reach your goal, you just know that if you consistently work towards it daily, you will arrive there at some point. It's really not rocket science; the formula is actually very simple. A well-laid plan+action+persistence and resilience= success. Along this journey, you never know what you will face from day to day. I have had to endure people lying on me, making attempts to assassinate my character, people that promised to be with me abandon me and leave me for dead. I have had to fight through my own thoughts of doubt and fear. And I have also experienced highs where people gravitated towards my offerings as well as periods where it felt as if nobody was checking for what I had to say, but one thing that I have learned is that each one of those experiences was all part of the process. Every one of those experiences has taught me something. Some things I learned about people, some things I learned about how to handle situations, but most of all, I learned a lot about me. As a result of having gone through all these, it has prepared me to handle the situations that will come my way in the future. Life is about learning, we must be lifelong learners, we must continue to evolve, and if we are smart, we must implement what we learn along the way. Enduring the process is not easy as you will experience highs as well as lows along the way, but the most critical thing to understand is that there are steps, and each one brings you closer to your ultimate goal or dream.

If there is anything that I could leave you with, it would be this; it is imperative to understand that nothing comes overnight and that things take time to build, there is a process to it all and no one is exempt from it. But if you remain diligent always assessing where you are, the process will prepare you in ways nothing else can. Learn to embrace the process and always look for the lesson in it so that you can use it to your benefit to consistently improve yourself. Keep your nose to the grind and always have faith that your efforts will not be in vain. You can and will make it if you do not give up and press towards your goal with relentless determination. Always expect to win, resting in the assurance that you will. And always, no matter what, stay committed to the resolve that failure is not an option!

Made in the USA
Lexington, KY
13 November 2019